Longman exam practice kit

GCSE
Science

Di Barton

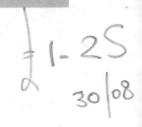

LONGMAN

SERIES EDITORS
Geoff Black and Stuart Wall

TITLES AVAILABLE

GCSE	A-level
Biology	Biology
Business Studies	Business Studies
English	Chemistry
Geography	Mathematics
Mathematics	Psychology
Physics	Sociology
Science	

Addison Wesley Longman Ltd.
Edinburgh Gate, Harlow,
Essex CM20 2JE, England
and Associated Companies throughout the World.

©Addison Wesley Longman 1997

First published 1997

ISBN 0582-30382-6

British Library Cataloguing-in-Publication Data
A catalogue record for this book is available from the British Library.

Typeset by 32 in 11/13pt Baskerville
Produced by Longman Asia Ltd, Hong Kong

Acknowledgements
We are grateful to the following exam boards for permission to reproduce
questions from past exam papers:

Midland Examining Group (MEG)
Northern Examinations and Assessment Board (NEAB)
Southern Examining Group (SEG)
University of London Examinations and Assessment Council (London) Now
    also known as EDEXCEL

Whilst every effort has been made to trace the owners of copyright material
we take this opportunity to offer our apologies to any copyright holders whose
rights we may have unwittingly infringed.

Contents

How to use this book — iv

Part I Preparing for the exam — **1**

A strategy for revision — 1

About the exam papers — 2

During the exam — 3

Assessment objectives in Science — 4

Part II Topic summaries and practice questions — **5**

Science 2: Life processes and living things

Chapter 1 The human body — 6

Chapter 2 Plants — 16

Chapter 3 Variation, inheritance and evolution — 22

Chapter 4 Ecology — 30

Science 3: Materials and their properties

Chapter 5 The periodic table, atomic structure and bonding — 38

Chapter 6 Useful products from oil and metals — 48

Chapter 7 Chemical reactions — 55

Chapter 8 The solar system; the Earth's geology and atmosphere — 61

Science 4: Physical processes

Chapter 9 Electricity and magnetism — 69

Chapter 10 Energy transfer and energy resources — 81

Chapter 11 Forces and motion — 85

Chapter 12 Waves — 93

Chapter 13 Radioactivity — 101

Part III Answers and grading — **107**

Part IV Timed practice paper with answers — **135**

How to use this book

This book seeks to help you achieve a good grade in your GCSE Science exam. It covers core topics which are common to all exam boards and some other topics that are very likely to be on your syllabus. The book is arranged in four parts.

Part I Preparing for the examination

This section covers what you should be doing before and during the examination. It gives advice about how to plan your revision, an explanation of the different types of examination question you might face and the assessment objectives in Science. A revision planner is also provided with this book to help you to structure your revision beginning some weeks before the examination.

Part II Topic areas, summaries and questions

This section has been split into 13 key topic areas which have been chosen to give you essential information to make your revision easier. In each area you will find:

1 **Topic outline and revision tips**   These will not replace your own full notes but will give you most of the basic facts that you need and present the material in short fact form that is easier to revise. If you need more detail the Longman Study Guide Science is a good source. Watch out for the **H** in the margin, these indicate that the bullet point or equation in the text beside the symbol will be expected by **Higher Tier** students only. There are also **HINTS** in the margin, giving you revision tips on particular topic areas.

2 **Practice questions**   The examination questions at the end of each topic are designed to test your knowledge of the topic area. It will help you to judge whether you need to spend more time revising that topic. The questions have been laid out in the same style as that of most examination boards, with spaces left for you to fill in your answers. Do make sure that you try to answer the questions before you look up the answers in the next section (Part III). Don't give up too easily or you aren't making the best use of the questions.

Part III All the answers

Here you will find answers to the practice questions. Use these to check your answers after you have attempted to answer the questions to your best ability. There are also student answers with examiner's notes to show where common mistakes are made.

Part IV Timed practice papers

This section contains a series of examination questions covering a variety of topics to give you practice in timing yourself under exam-type conditions before the examination. Examiner's notes are again provided for each question so that you can see how well you have performed.

This book will help you to:

- organise your Science notes into topics,
- identify key facts,
- prepare for your Science exam,
- learn how to gain marks when answering questions,
- try past exam questions and check your answers against those given,
- see how other students have tried past questions and learn from the examiner's comments on their work,
- time yourself in a practice exam paper and mark your work against the answers and marking guidelines given.

part I

Preparing for the exam

A STRATEGY FOR REVISION

Organise your notes

1   **Organise your Science notes into the three main areas.**

   ▶ Sc 2: *Life processes and living things* (Biology)
   ▶ Sc 3: *Materials and their properties* (Chemistry)
   ▶ Sc 4: *Physical processes* (Physics)

   These match the three examination papers offered by most Examining Groups. You may have been taught by one teacher for all of these, or by three or more teachers specialising in different topics. It is important now that your notes are organised into the main areas to help you structure your revision into 'bite-sized' chunks!

> **HINT**
> *Use the Contents list at the front of this book as a guide. Don't worry if your list differs from the Contents list; there are different ways of dividing up the topics in the syllabus; all that matters is that you have your own list of topics*

2   **Make a list of the main topics within each of these three areas.**
   You should have about 12–16 topic headings, for example, *Humans, Chemical reactions, Forces and motion.*

3   **Arrange your notes so they match your topic headings.**

   ▶ Write at the top of each page of notes the topic it fits into, or use a number system Sc 2.1, Sc 2.2, etc.
   ▶ If you are missing any notes through being absent, now is the time to photocopy a friend's notes, or ask your teacher for help.
   ▶ Don't worry if some of your notes don't match the topic list exactly; there may have been some variation in your Science course, for example, 'Radioactivity' may have been taught in Chemistry or Physics, 'The Earth's Geology' may have been covered as a separate unit or combined with another.

> **HINT**
> *All that matters is that these topics are listed somewhere!*

4   **Make your notes work for you.**

   ▶ Go through your notes using a highlighter or coloured pens to mark all subheadings: for example in the topic 'The human body' the subheadings might be: *Nutrition, Circulation*, etc.
   ▶ Tick any topics you are really confident about and mark those that will need extra revision; try using a star system to code each topic, say * easy, ** OK, *** hard.

> **HINT**
> *Use the subheadings in the topic summaries in this book to help you*

Plan your revision

   ▶ Use the Revision planner provided with this book or draw up your own timetable showing the number of days and weeks before the exam; don't forget to mark in any other commitments: sports, social events, etc!

HINT

Of course, you'll have all your other subjects to revise as well and will still need some time for exercise and relaxation!

▶ Divide your 15 or so main topics between the number of days/weeks you have before the exam.
▶ You might aim to revise two or three topics a week (for example *The periodic table*, *Waves*, *Ecology*) for the seven or eight weeks before the exams start.
▶ If you have time it may help to divide the bigger topics into two or three subheadings and revise one a day!

Make your revision active

Turning over pages of notes is very passive (and boring); how much can you really remember of the previous page? An active and more stimulating strategy is to:

▶ Use a highlighter to mark *key facts* in a topic, then see how much you can remember!
▶ Start the next day's revision session with a *memory test* on the previous day's key facts; this is *active revision*.
▶ Learn the labels on diagrams by covering the labels with a piece of paper and then seeing how many you can remember; this is also active revision.
▶ Draw a flow chart, e.g. the carbon cycle, and see how many blank spaces you can complete.
▶ Refer to the topic summaries in Part II of this book; add to them if necessary.
▶ Make your own *summary of key facts* in some topics on plain card to give you a useful set of key fact cards; you can look at these a few days before the exam when there's little time left!

Use exam questions in revision

At the end of each topic summary in this book there are two to five practice questions taken from GCSE Key Stage 4 exam papers set by the Examining Groups; when you have revised a topic *test yourself* by answering one or two questions and then mark your answers with the help of the answers and mark scheme in Part III; there are examiner's comments throughout the answers to help you to understand how an answer gains marks, as well as showing you how to find clues to the answers within the questions.

ABOUT THE EXAM PAPERS

▶ The exam papers are taken at the end of the GCSE course, usually during May or June.
▶ There are two tiers of exam papers: *Foundation Tier* for grades C to G and *Higher Tier* for grades A* to D; you only enter for one tier so make sure you are entered for the tier that realistically reflects your ability; some questions are common to both tiers but there may be more difficult parts added on the Higher Tier paper.
▶ There are usually three papers of about $1\frac{1}{2}$–2 hours, usually one paper for each main area: Sc 2 *Life processes and living things*, Sc 3 *Materials and their properties*, and Sc 4 *Physical processes*.
▶ The papers are each worth about 100 marks; the number of questions varies from year to year but is usually between 8 and 12. Together the papers are worth 75% of your total mark (50% on modular courses); the other 25% is from coursework. The number of marks for each subquestion is clearly shown in brackets.

HINT

If you gain below grade D on the Higher Tier papers you are ungraded

Types of exam question

The papers all contain compulsory questions, answered on the question paper in the spaces provided; there are four styles of question used:

1 *short answer questions:* answered in a sentence or even a few words;
2 *structured questions:* start with an introductory sentence followed by stimulus material (a diagram or table of information) and then a series of short subquestions (a) (b) (c) connected by a common theme; you are given guidance as to the type and length of answer required;
3 *questions requiring extended writing:* need more writing and a wider use of language; they may ask you to 'explain how something happens' or to 'suggest reasons for your answer';
4 *open-ended free-response questions:* provide little or no structure for the answer but just allocate several lines of space.

> **HINT**
> If you cannot do part (a) go on to part (b)

> **HINT**
> Extended prose and free-response questions are frequently used on Higher Tier papers

DURING THE EXAM

▶ Aim to fill the space provided; and if the question asks for 'two reasons' make sure you give two and not just one!
▶ Use as many scientific words as possible to show the examiner how much you know; remember the topic summaries and your key facts.
▶ Check that the number of marks allocated in brackets matches the number of facts you have written.
▶ If you are asked for a calculation, always write the formula and state the units: for example, N (newtons) or J (joules).
▶ Watch your time: if the paper is worth 100 marks and you have $1\frac{1}{2}$ hours (90 minutes) then, allowing time for checking, you need to aim for a mark a minute! Check how many marks are allocated to the question and don't spend longer than that amount of time in minutes.
▶ At the end of the paper don't just gaze out of the window; use every available minute to check and add to your answers; try the subquestions you may have missed out; even one or two extra marks may help you gain a higher grade!

> **HINT**
> There are often scientific words used in the question which can help your answer

> **HINT**
> Remember one correct fact usually gains 1 mark

> **HINT**
> 10 marks means about 10 minutes of time

Words of instruction used in exam questions

In exam questions there is usually a 'word of instruction' in each subquestion; this tells you how to answer the question in a certain way: for example, if you are asked to 'explain' then writing a description will not gain the marks.

One syllabus describes four groups of words of instruction (depending on the context some words may appear in more than one group):

1 *state..., list..., name..., what..., how..., describe..., what is meant by...*
These words are about *recall of information* (roughly 20% of the exam will test factual recall), for example: '*Name* the part labelled A on the line provided'; '*What* is the function of valve D?'; '*State* the feature you can see on the diagram'.

2 *explain..., complete..., why..., construct..., which...*
These words are about using recalled information in a *wider context*, for example: '*Explain* why the wall of the left ventricle is more muscular...'; '*Explain* the advantages of using...'; '*Complete* the table by writing in the space provided'.

3 *suggest..., work out..., how would you know that...*
These words assess your ability in *problem solving, interpretation, evaluation, data handling* and in *communication* of scientific ideas and principles. '*Suggest*' is one of the most commonly used words, for example: '*Suggest* two reasons why'; '*Suggest* how this change could have happened'.

HINT

It may be helpful to identify and underline the word(s) of instruction in the question before you start to answer

4   *calculate…,   predict…,   discuss…*

These words are usually used on Higher Tier papers and ask you to *apply knowledge, interpret, evaluate* and *process information,* for example: '*Calculate* John's acceleration between points X and Y'.

ASSESSMENT OBJECTIVES IN SCIENCE

Assessment objectives state the skills and abilities which you should develop as a result of studying Science; you will be assessed on these objectives by coursework and in the written exam. There are three main assessment objectives:

1 *experimental and investigative Science* (25%)
2 *knowledge and understanding* (60%, about one-third for recall)
3 *communication and evaluation* (15%)

The second and third objectives are relevant to Sc 2, Sc 3 and Sc 4.

▶ Knowledge and understanding (60%):
   recall, understand, use and apply the scientific knowledge set out in the syllabus (about one-third recall)

▶ Communication and evaluation (15%):
   communicate scientific observations, ideas and arguments using a range of scientific and technical vocabulary and appropriate scientific and mathematical conventions; evaluate relevant scientific information and make informed judgements from it

The target weighting for the assessment of *recall* (remembering facts) is 20–25%; it is important that you as a candidate realise that the written exam paper is not going to test only recall of facts but also your *understanding* and *application* of those facts, as well as your ability to *communicate.*

part II

Topic summaries and practice questions

The human body

1 Nutrition

Digestion is the breakdown of large insoluble molecules into small soluble molecules which can pass into the blood stream.

Structure of the human digestive system – learn where these parts are and their function:

▶ **salivary glands** produce saliva and amylases
▶ **oesophagus** through which food passes by peristalsis
▶ **stomach** produces dilute hydrochloric acid and proteases
▶ **small intestine** where small molecules are absorbed into the blood stream
▶ **large intestine** absorbs water and faeces
▶ **pancreas** produces insulin and lipases
▶ **liver** stores excess sugar as glycogen
▶ **gall bladder** stores bile which emulsifies fats

> **HINT**
> *Place a piece of paper over the labels on each side of the diagram and write the names and functions from memory*

Figure 1.1
The human digestive system

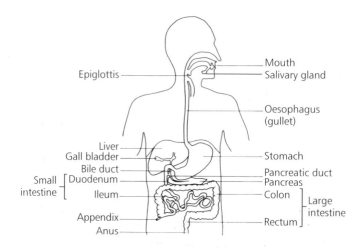

After breakdown, the small soluble molecules pass through the **villi** into the blood stream. **Enzymes** increase the rate of breakdown:

▶ **amylase** changes starch to sugar
▶ **proteases** change protein to amino acids
▶ **lipases** change fats to fatty acids and glycerol

Figure 1.2
The villi in the small intestine increase the area for absorption

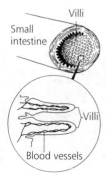

2 Circulation

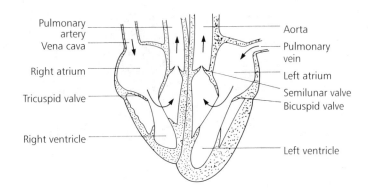

Figure 1.3
The heart is a powerful pump which pumps blood around the body and to the lungs

> **HINT**
> *Check what you know by covering up the labels on the diagram of the heart*

> **HINT**
> *Remember thick-walled arteries carry blood away from the heart under pressure*

▶ The **aorta** carries oxygenated blood round the body; the **pulmonary artery** carries deoxygenated blood to the lungs; the **vena cava** carries deoxygenated blood to the heart.

▶ The **heart** is a muscular double pump: the *right* side pumps blood to the lungs at low pressure; the *left* side pumps blood to the body at higher pressure.

▶ The **ventricles** contract to pump blood; the *left* ventricle has a thicker muscular wall than the right ventricle as blood is pumped to body organs via the aorta.

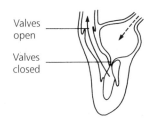

Figure 1.4
The heart in action

Ventricle relaxed: blood is forced from the atrium into the ventricle. Valves prevent blood flowing 'backwards'

Ventricle contracted: blood is forced from the ventricle and out of the heart. The atrium meanwhile re-fills with more blood

▶ **Valves** in the veins and the heart ensure one-way flow of blood.

▶ **Red cells** in the blood contain **haemoglobin** and carry oxygen; **white cells** ingest bacteria and produce antibodies; **platelets** help in clotting.

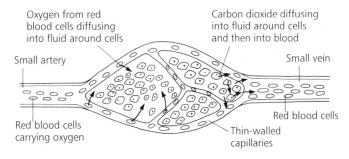

Figure 1.5
Oxygen diffuses into the tissue fluid around cells

3 Breathing

> **HINT**
> *Check your knowledge using the diagram of the thorax on page 8*

▶ Learn: **trachea, alveoli, lungs, intercostal muscles, diaphragm** and **ribs**.

▶ **Ventilation** (breathing in) – the intercostals contract, the ribs move up and out, the diaphragm contracts and flattens, warm moist air rushes into the lungs where **gaseous exchange** occurs: **oxygen** diffuses over the thin moist surface of the alveoli into **capillaries** and combines with haemoglobin of red blood cells, and **carbon dioxide** diffuses out of the blood.

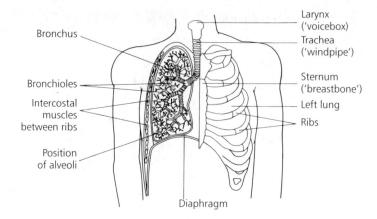

Figure 1.6
The human thorax
(chest cavity)

▶ Inhalation of **carbon monoxide** reduces the oxygen-carrying capacity of blood.

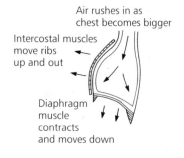

Figure 1.7a
Breathing in

Figure 1.7b
Breathing out

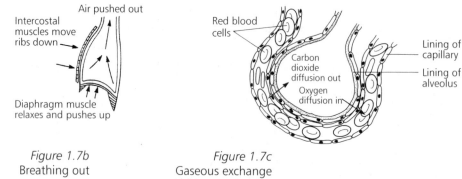

Figure 1.7c
Gaseous exchange
inside one alveolus

4 Respiration

▶ **Aerobic** respiration is the release of energy using oxygen:

glucose + oxygen $\longrightarrow$ carbon dioxide + water + (energy transferred)

Ⓗ $C_6H_{12}O_6 + 6O_2 \longrightarrow 6CO_2 + 6H_2O$ + (energy transferred)

▶ **Anaerobic** respiration is the release of energy without using oxygen:

glucose $\longrightarrow$ alcohol + (energy transferred)

▶ Oxygen debt results from muscles respiring anaerobically during vigorous exercise and producing lactic acid.

5 Nervous system

A **reflex action** is a rapid automatic response to a stimulus.

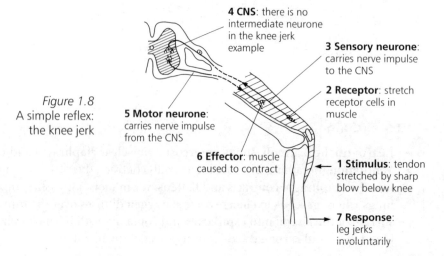

Figure 1.8
A simple reflex:
the knee jerk

Sense organs contain receptors:

- ear – sound and balance
- eye – sight
- tongue – taste (chemicals)
- skin – touch and temperature

When a stimulus is detected a nerve impulse (electrical signal) is transmitted along **neurones** (nerve cells) and across **synapses** (gaps between nerve cells) to the brain and spinal cord (the **central nervous system, CNS**), then along neurones to **effector muscles** which carry out a response:

$$\text{stimulus} \longrightarrow \text{receptor} \longrightarrow \text{neurones} \longrightarrow \text{effector} \longrightarrow \text{response}$$

The eye
Learn the name and function of:

- **cornea**, **ciliary muscles** and **lens** all for focusing
- **retina** light-sensitive layer of rods which function in dim light, and cones which detect colour and detail
- **iris** controls amount of light entering eye through pupil and reaching retina
- **optic nerve** carries impulses from retina to brain

In image formation light rays are refracted (bent) by the cornea and the lens and focused on the retina where an inverted (upside-down) image is formed.

Figure 1.9
The structure of the eye

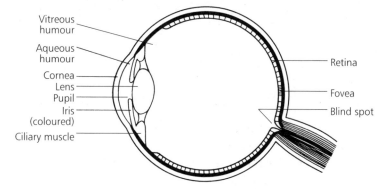

The ear
This is dealt with in Topic 11 (p. 96).

6 Hormones

Hormones are substances secreted by **endocrine glands** and carried in the blood plasma to target cells in organs. Some hormones you should be familiar with are:

- **Oestrogen** and **progesterone** (in the female) or **testosterone** (in the male) – control physical changes during puberty. They are used to artificially control and promote fertility.
- **(H)** **Insulin** – produced by the pancreas and controls the level of blood sugar, by removing glucose from the blood stream and assisting the conversion of glucose into glycogen in the liver. It is used by diabetics to artificially control blood sugar levels.

7 Homeostasis

Homeostasis is the maintenance of a steady internal environment. This means that to enable cells to function efficiently, the tissue fluid around the cells must be kept at a constant composition. Two factors can be considered: *water content* (via the excretory system) and *temperature control* (via the skin).

The excretory system

The excretory system performs two main functions: *removal of toxic waste substances* produced by reactions in the cells and *control of the body's water content*.

Identify these parts of the excretory system and state their function:

▶ **kidneys** – filtration, reabsorption
▶ **renal artery** and **vein** – blood supply to and from kidneys
▶ **ureter** – carries urine to bladder
▶ **bladder** – storage of urine
▶ **urethra** – transport of urine out of the body

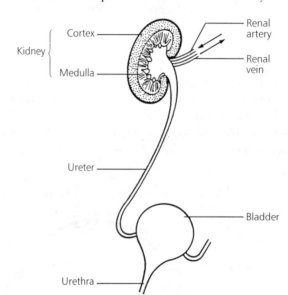

Figure 1.10
The excretory system

Kidney structure – learn the following terms:

▶ **nephron** (kidney tubule)
▶ **renal capsule**
▶ **renal tubule**
▶ **collecting duct**

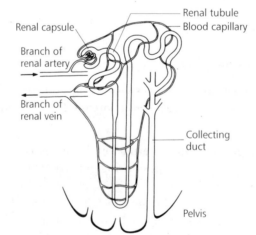

Figure 1.11
A nephron

The function of the kidneys

Two important functions of the kidneys are *removal of urea* and *control of fluid balance* (regulation of the water content of the blood).

▶ In the kidneys blood with a high concentration of **urea** is filtered (sieved) at high pressure (ultra-filtration) through the renal capsule into the renal tubule; the urea remains in the urine but water and some salts are selectively reabsorbed from the tubule into the blood as required.

▶ If there is too little water in the blood (due to urination and/or sweating), more **ADH** (a hormone) is released by the **pituitary gland** in the brain and causes the kidneys to reabsorb as much water as possible so a small volume of concentrated urine is produced; the person also feels thirsty and drinks more. If there is too much water in the blood (from drinking) then less ADH is released and the kidneys produce a large volume of dilute urine.

People whose kidneys fail to work are treated either by dialysis or transplant.

▶ A **dialysis machine** (artificial kidney) filters the blood and removes urea and some salts; dialysis can take several hours 2–3 days a week and is very costly.

▶ A **kidney transplant** usually involves a long wait for a kidney from a donor as there are insufficient donors to meet demands; there may be rejection of the new kidney by the body's immune system.

Temperature control

Temperature control is carried out by the skin. **In warm weather**:

▶ sweating is increased, heat is taken from the body to evaporate sweat and the body feels cooler;

▶ **vasodilation** occurs: the blood capillaries dilate (widen) to increase heat loss.

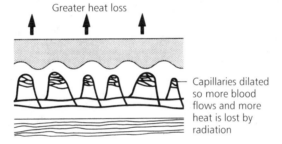

Figure 1.12a
Vasodilation

In cooler weather:

▶ sweating decreases to reduce heat loss;

▶ **vasoconstriction** occurs: the blood capillaries constrict (narrow) to reduce heat loss.

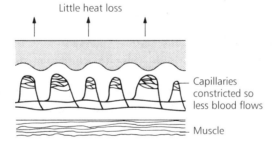

Figure 1.12b
Vasoconstriction

8 Health

The outer layers of the skin prevent harmful **bacteria** reaching living tissue. White blood cells also act as **defence mechanisms**: they engulf bacteria in the blood, form **antibodies** to destroy bacteria, and produce **antitoxins** to neutralise toxins produced by bacteria.

Use and misuse of drugs

Drugs can be beneficial but are harmful if misused. Some commonly misused drugs and their effects are:

▶ **Depressants** and **stimulants** – often obtained illegally; there is no control over their strength or quality (they may be mixed with impure chemicals to increase bulk); there are no guidelines on dosage; they can cause behaviour changes and damage to liver, brain and kidneys; an associated risk is through use of shared needles (unsterilised) which can lead to blood poisoning, hepatitis and HIV.

▶ **Alcohol** – affects the nervous system and slows down reaction time; excess may lead to increased aggressive behaviour.

▶ **Nicotine** in tobacco smoke – this is **addictive** (habit forming) and affects the nervous system.

▶ **Solvent abuse** (glue sniffing) – causes sores around the mouth and eyes; leads to moody, irritable behaviour; is very addictive; affects brain and can lead to unconsciousness and death.

PRACTICE QUESTIONS

Question 1

The diagrams below show a section through the **left** side of a human heart during two stages of a heart beat.

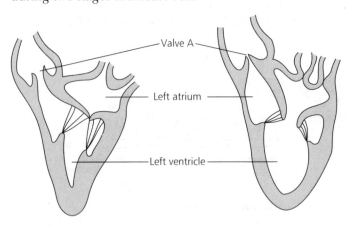

(a) Place an arrow on *each* diagram to show the direction of blood flow in the heart during the stages shown.   (2)

(b) What is the function of valve **A**, labelled on the diagram?

....

....(2)

(c) Name the vessel bringing blood to the left atrium.

....(1)

(d) Explain why the wall of the left ventricle is more muscular than the wall of the left atrium.

....

....(1)

(Total marks 6)

London

Question 2

A scientist took some measurements of air breathed in and out by an athlete. The table shows the percentage of gases in the air samples.

Gas	Air breathed in / %	Air breathed out / %
Oxygen	20	16
Carbon dioxide	0.04	4
Nitrogen	79	79

(a) Explain the reason for the difference in the amounts of oxygen and carbon dioxide in the two samples.

....

....

....

....(2)

(b) Why does the percentage of nitrogen remain constant in the two samples?

....(1)

When the athlete exercises vigorously her muscles build up an 'oxygen debt'.

(c) Complete the word equation for anaerobic respiration in a muscle cell.

glucose ⟶ .... + energy   (1)

(d) Explain why the ability to build up an oxygen debt is an advantage to an athlete.

....

....

....

....(2)

(Total marks 6)

MEG

Question 3

The diagram represents the structure of a nephron from a kidney of a human.

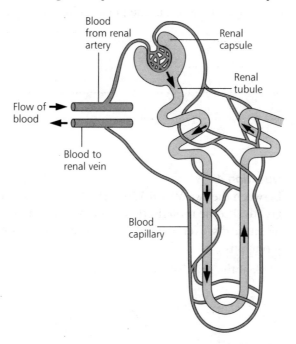

Source: adapted from MICHAEL ROBERTS, *The Living World* (Nelson)

(a) The table shows the results of measuring the concentrations of two substances in three different parts of a nephron.

Substance	Concentration (measured in g per 100 cm³)		
	In the blood in the renal artery	In the renal capsule	In the urine
Protein	7.0	0.0	0.0
Urea	0.03	0.03	2.0

(i) No protein is present in the contents of the renal capsule. Explain why.

....

....

....(3)

(ii) [A] Why do our bodies need to get rid of urea?

....(1)

[B] The concentration of urea in urine is higher than elsewhere in the kidney. Explain why.

....(1)

(b) The diagram represents an artificial kidney machine. Kidney machines are used by people whose own kidneys stop working. The machine works by a process called dialysis.

Dialysis solution

Blood to
patient's
vein

Blood from
patient's
vein

Tube of dialysing
membrane

Dialysis solution
+
Waste from the blood

It is important that the dialysis solution contains glucose at the same concentration as it is in the person's blood. Explain why.

....

....

....

....(3)

(Total marks 8)

SEG

Question 4

Between the two World Wars (1914–1939) sales of tobacco in Britain increased greatly. People thought that smoking tobacco was harmless. In the 1960s scientists discovered a link between smoking and lung diseases such as bronchitis.

Look at the graphs below.

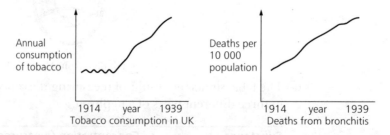

Annual
consumption
of tobacco

1914   year   1939
Tobacco consumption in UK

Deaths per
10 000
population

1914   year   1939
Deaths from bronchitis

(a) Explain how the evidence in the graphs supports the idea that smoking is harmful to health.

....

....(1)

(b) Smokers are advised to reduce their intake of tobacco.

Why is it difficult for people to give up smoking?

....

...................................:...(2)

(c) The diagrams show sections of an artery from a non-smoker and a smoker.

Artery from a non-smoker   Artery from a smoker

Muscle wall

(i)   Describe how the structure of an artery is related to its function.

....

....

....(3)

(ii)   Use the diagrams to explain how smoking may lead to the onset of heart disease.

....

....

....(3)

(d) Cigarette smoke contains carbon monoxide. This combines strongly with haemoglobin in the red blood cells.

How will this affect a person who smokes heavily?

....

....

(2)

(Total marks 11)

MEG

2 Plants

TOPIC OUTLINE AND REVISION TIPS

1 Life processes and cell activity

> **HINT**
> *The first letter of each of these can make an easy-to-remember nonsense phrase:* **m**any **n**aughty **r**abbits **e**at **g**reen **r**hubarb **s**hoots

There are seven life processes common to all animals and plants: *movement*, *nutrition*, *respiration*, *excretion*, *growth*, *reproduction*, *sensitivity*.

All plant and animal cells contain:

▶ a **nucleus** contains chromosomes which carry all genetic material as DNA
▶ a **cell membrane** allows movement of substances in and out of the cell
▶ **cytoplasm** where enzyme-controlled reactions take place
▶ **mitochondria** where energy is transferred; these can only be seen using an electron microscope

Only plant cells contain a **cell wall** (a tough outer layer made of cellulose; it is rigid and keeps the shape of the cell regular); **chloroplast** (contains a green chemical **chlorophyll**, which traps light energy enabling **photosynthesis**); a permanent **vacuole** (stores water, sugar and minerals; this helps to support the plant, preventing wilting).

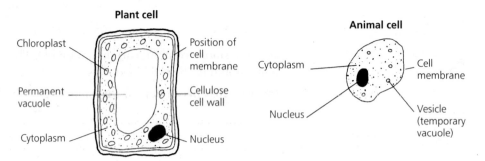

Figure 2.1
Generalised plant and animal cells

The table shows the differences between plant and animal cells.

Feature	Plant cell	Animal cell
Cell wall	Present	Absent
Cell vacuole	Large permanent vacuole	Small temporary vesicle
Chloroplast	Present	Absent
Shape of cell	Regular	Irregular

2 Nutrition

Learn the equation for **photosynthesis** and be able to explain the process.

$$\text{carbon dioxide} + \text{water} \xrightarrow[\text{light energy}]{\text{chlorophyll}} \text{glucose} + \text{oxygen}$$

$$6CO_2 + 6H_2O \longrightarrow C_6H_{12}O_6 + 6O_2$$

▶ Light energy comes from the Sun.
▶ **Chlorophyll** (the green pigment stored in the **chloroplasts**) absorbs light energy for the process of photosynthesis.

HINT
*Look up in your practical notes
any investigations into
photosynthesis; remember the
importance of destarching a
plant to use up the starch
before doing an investigation*

▶ **Glucose** is converted to **starch** and other products and is stored.
▶ **Oxygen** is released as a waste product; it is used for **respiration** by animals and plants.

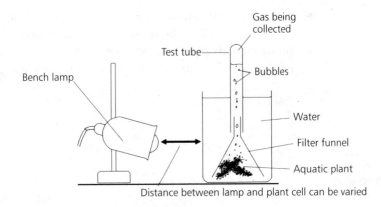

Figure 2.2a
Experiment to
demonstrate the effect
of light intensity on the
rate of photosynthesis

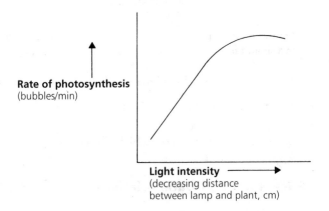

Figure 2.2b
Graph to show the
effect of light intensity
on the rate of
photosynthesis

 Limiting factors prevent the rate of photosynthesis from increasing. These factors are:

▶ *light intensity* and *duration*
▶ *carbon dioxide concentration*
▶ *temperature*

Glucose produced by photosynthesis is used as a **source of energy**. Glucose is converted to:

▶ **starch** stored in roots and stems
▶ **sucrose** stored in fruit
▶ **oils** stored in seeds for germination
▶ **amino acids** used for making proteins in growth

3 Mineral salts

These are used by plants to help manufacture **proteins** and other substances (oxygen, hydrogen and carbon are also necessary).

Mineral	Needed for	Symptom due to lack of mineral
Nitrogen	To make amino acids, proteins and DNA	Small leaves, thin weak stems
Phosphorus	To make DNA and cell membranes, and for enzyme systems	Poor root growth, small leaves
Magnesium	To make chlorophyll	Yellow leaves

4 Hormones

(H) **Auxins** are plant hormones which stimulate or inhibit growth. They are released by shoots and root tip in one of two ways:

▶ positive **phototropism** – auxin accumulates on the side *away* from light and *stimulates* growth so the shoot grows *towards* light;
▶ positive **geotropism** – auxin accumulates on the *lower* side of the root and *inhibits* growth so the root responds to gravity and grows *downwards*.

Figure 2.3
Role of auxin in growth
of shoots and roots

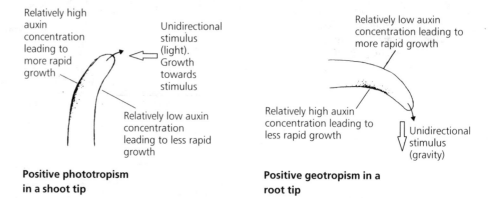

Positive phototropism in a shoot tip

Positive geotropism in a root tip

Commercially produced growth hormones are used to stimulate:

▶ *fruit formation* without fertilisation
▶ *root growth* in cuttings
▶ *fast growth of specific weeds* which then die

5 Transport and water relations

Osmosis

Osmosis is the diffusion of water molecules from a region of higher water concentration to one of lower water concentration through a partially permeable membrane (for example, the cell membrane).

(H) ▶ Water moves into the root by osmosis.
▶ Root hairs increase the surface area for absorption of water.
▶ Water and mineral salts are transported through the **xylem** to the leaf.

Figure 2.4a–c
Distribution of vascular
tissues in a
dicotyledonous plant
(vertical and transverse
sections)

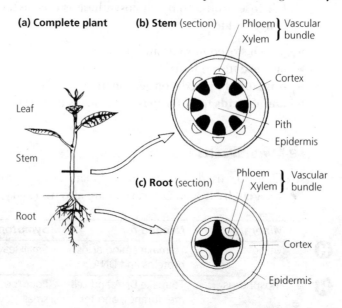

When the plant has sufficient water the cells become **turgid** (swollen); when the plant loses excessive water by **transpiration** and is unable to take in sufficient water the cells become **flaccid**; the plant wilts and is unable to photosynthesise.

Transpiration

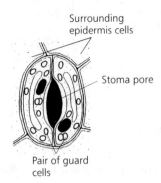

Figure 2.5
A stoma showing two
guard cells

Transpiration is the loss of water vapour by evaporation. Plants lose water by transpiration through **stomata** (tiny holes or pores). Stomata are the main route for the movement of gases into and out of the leaf. Each stoma can be opened or closed by changes in the shape of the **guard cells**. Transpiration is increased by:

▶ increase in *light intensity*
▶ increase in *temperature*
▶ increase in *air movement*
▶ decrease in *humidity*

 PRACTICE QUESTIONS

Question 1
Photosynthesis takes place in the green leaves of plants.

(a) Write down the word equation which represents photosynthesis.

....(2)

(b) Four test tubes, **A**, **B**, **C** and **D**, were set up as shown, and left in *darkness* for 24 hours.

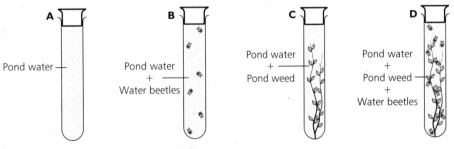

After being in the dark for 24 hours the amounts of oxygen in the water were compared.

In which test tube would there be *most* oxygen in the water? Give a reason for your choice.

Test tube ...., because ....

....

....(3)

(c) Four test tubes, **W**, **X**, **Y** and **Z**, were set up as shown. These were left in the *light* for 24 hours.

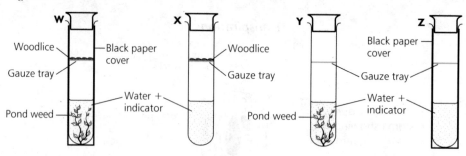

The indicator in each test tube turns from orange to yellow when the amount of carbon dioxide increases.

In which test tube would the indicator turn yellow *first*? Give a reason for your choice.

Test tube ...., because ....

....

....(3)

(Total marks 8)
SEG

Question 2

The drawing shows a root hair cell from near the tip of a young root.

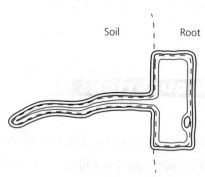

(a) This cell needs oxygen. Name the process by which oxygen enters the cell from the air in the soil.

....(1)

(b) Describe the process by which water enters the root hair cells.

....

....

....

....(3)

(c) A seaside garden is flooded by the sea in an exceptionally severe storm. Several of the plants wilt and die.

Explain why flooding with sea water caused the plants to wilt.

....

....

....

....(2)

(Total 6)
NEAB

Question 3

(a) Complete the equation for photosynthesis

carbon dioxide + ... + light energy ⟶ sugar + ... (2)

(b) A plant with variegated (two coloured) leaves was left in sunlight for several hours. Pieces of one of its leaves were then removed and tested for sugar. The diagram shows the results of the test.

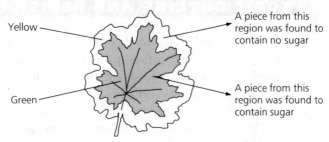

Yellow

Green

A piece from this region was found to contain no sugar

A piece from this region was found to contain sugar

Explain, as fully as you can, why the yellow regions of the leaf had not produced sugar.

....

....

....

....(3)

(c) Explain why plants need nitrate and potassium for healthy growth.

1. nitrate

....(1)

2. potassium

....

....(2)

(Total marks 8)

NEAB

Variation, inheritance and evolution

✓ TOPIC OUTLINE AND REVISION TIPS

You may have studied the first section of this topic, **variation**, under separate headings such as growth, reproduction and mutations. In whatever way your notes are arranged, you should be able to link reproduction and growth with cell division (meiosis and mitosis) and have an understanding of chromosomes and genes, genetic engineering and mutations.

The second section of this topic, **inheritance**, explains how characteristics are inherited by individuals through the mechanism of the monohybrid cross and how this knowledge can be applied to selective breeding.

The third section is concerned with **evolution**, the importance of the fossil record and Darwin's ideas on natural selection.

1 Variation

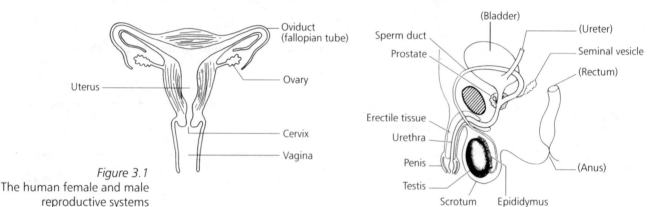

Figure 3.1
The human female and male reproductive systems

HINT
Place a piece of paper over the labels at the side of these diagrams of the male and female reproductive systems and try to write the labels from memory

Identify and state the function of:

▶ **testes, sperm tubes, urethra, penis, scrotum**
▶ **ovaries, oviducts, uterus, cervix** and **vagina**

Cell division
Cell division may be by **meiosis** or **mitosis**.

Meiosis	Mitosis
Non-identical cells, gametes, formed (egg and sperm)	Exact genetic copies of chromosomes made before cell division to produce identical cells; used for growth, e.g. to form new body cells
Half (haploid) chromosome number	Full (diploid) chromosome number

H

Figure 3.2a
Mitosis in a cell with four chromosomes

      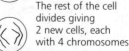

The rest of the cell divides giving 2 new cells, each with 4 chromosomes

2 pairs of chromosomes   They double   and separate into 2 groups

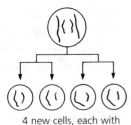

Figure 3.2b
Meiosis in a cell with
four chromosomes

4 new cells, each with
only 2 chromosomes

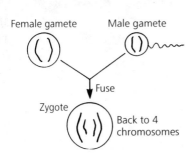

Figure 3.2c
Fertilisation

Fertilisation

Fertilisation is the fusion of **haploid gametes** (an egg by the sperm) to form a **zygote** which has the full (**diploid**) number of chromosomes (23 pairs in humans).

▶ The random fusion of gametes causes **genetic variation** in offspring due to random combination of chromosomes in meiosis.

▶ Identical twins are formed from one fertilised egg which divides by mitosis into two separate embryos.

▶ Non-identical twins are formed when two sperm fertilise two eggs at the same time.

▶ **Clones** are genetically identical offspring formed as a result of mitosis during asexual reproduction.

▶ The nucleus of a cell contains **chromosomes**, long molecules of **DNA** divided into **genes** which carry genetic information; alternative forms of genes are **alleles**; these cause variation among individuals.

▶ **Continuous variation**, e.g. in height can be caused by the interaction of genetic factors with environmental factors such as availability of food in the case of animals, or availability of light, minerals etc. in the case of plants.

Figure 3.3
Discontinuous and
continuous variation

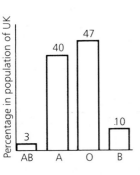

**Discontinuous variation
in human blood groups**

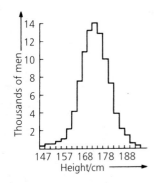

**Continuous variation
in humans: height**

▶ **DNA** is a complex molecule composed of two strands coiled to form a double helix; the strands are linked by paired bases (adenine with thymine and cytosine with guanine); it is the sequence of these bases within a gene that directs the sequence in which amino acids are made to form particular proteins: *one gene – one protein.*

Genetic engineering

This is the insertion of new genes into the DNA of bacteria, using enzymes, to make genetically altered cells which produce useful substances, e.g. human insulin.

Mutations

These are caused by errors in copying genes and chromosomes during cell division; mutations can be increased by exposure to radiation (gamma rays, X-rays and UV rays) and some chemicals. Some mutations are harmful, some neutral and some beneficial. For example, the sickle cell gene causes sickle-shaped red blood cells which give some immunity to malaria although the person is anaemic. Other examples of inherited (genetic) diseases are cystic fibrosis, muscular dystrophy and haemophilia.

2 Inheritance

▶ Sex determination results from the fusion of:

    X egg with X sperm = **female XX** (gametes are all X)

    X egg with Y sperm = **male XY** (50% gametes are X, 50% are Y)

▶ **Homozygous** means having two *identical alleles* for a gene – two dominant or two recessive.

▶ **Heterozygous** means having two *different alleles* for a gene – one dominant and one recessive.

▶ **Genotype** is the *genetic* constitution of an individual.

▶ **Phenotype** is the *physical* appearance of the individual determined by the interaction of the genetic constitution and the environment.

Ⓗ The mechanisms of monohybrid inheritance

Consider a monohybrid genetic cross involving *one pair of alleles* and two parents, for example a genetic cross involving the alleles for eye colour where brown is dominant to blue. If both parents are brown-eyed but are heterozygous for eye colour, they have the dominant allele for brown eye colour and the recessive allele for blue eye colour.

Write out the genetic cross like this (state the letters you are going to use):

```
Let B be the symbol for brown and b be the symbol for blue.
   parent's genotype  Bb  X  Bb
   gametes            B  b  X  B  b
```

```
Offspring (F₁) genotypes are shown in a checkerboard diagram:
```

Gametes	B	B
B	BB	Bb
b	Bb	bb

```
Offspring (F₁) phenotypes are:
   BB brown eyes (homozygous)
   Bb brown eyes (heterozygous)
   bb blue eyes (homozygous)
```

There is a 3:1 ratio of brown to blue eyes which means a 25% probability of a child inheriting blue eyes from these parents.

Knowledge of monohybrid inheritance put to use

▶ **Selective breeding** develops crop plants and agricultural animals which have favourable characteristics (traits) such as good yields and resistance to drought and disease; plants and animals with desirable traits are crossed (mated) and those offspring with the same desirable traits are used for breeding the next generation and so on.

▶ **Cloning** can be used to produce identical copies of the same individuals with desirable characteristics; techniques used involve taking cuttings of plants.
▶ **Genes** which make useful proteins can be transferred from the chromosomes of humans and other organisms and inserted into the DNA of bacterial cells. The transferred gene continues to make the same protein, for example insulin. By culturing the bacteria on a large scale, commercial quantities can be produced.

3 Evolution

Evolution is a series of changes in the appearance of animals and plants over millions of years. Evolution can be observed in the incomplete **fossil record** of some organisms such as the horse; bones from early ancestors of the horse have become fossilised in sedimentary rocks which can be dated.

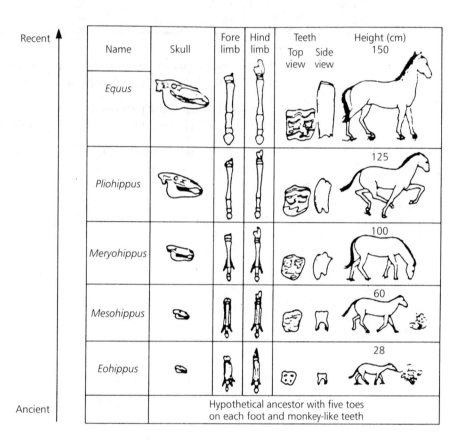

Figure 3.4
Evolution of the horse

Darwin's theory of natural selection
Darwin made four observations on which he based his theory of **natural selection**:

1 organisms produce large numbers of offspring;
2 population numbers remain fairly constant over a period of time;
3 there is variation among the offspring;
4 some of the variations are inherited.

Natural selection leads to certain alleles becoming more or less common. This means that those organisms which have *favourable variations* may survive to breed and pass on their favourable traits to the next generation and so on; these organisms are usually better able to adapt to any environmental changes.

The organisms which have *less favourable traits* are often weaker and many die due to predators, disease, lack of food etc.; they may be less able to adapt to any changes in the environment.

PRACTICE QUESTIONS

Question 1

(a) There are important differences between cell divisions producing body cells and cell divisions producing egg or sperm cells.

For a cell with 12 chromosomes, show in the table:

(i) the number of cells formed from the single original cell;

(ii) the number of chromosomes in each new nucleus.

	Cell dividing to form new body cells	Cell dividing to form egg or sperm cells
(i) Number of cells formed		
(ii) Number of chromosomes		

(2)

(b) Chromosomes passed by the egg or sperm cell to the next generation may carry genes for inherited diseases such as Huntington's chorea.

In a family, one of the parents carries a single dominant allele for Huntington's chorea. The other parent carries two recessive alleles.

Use a genetic diagram to work out the probability of any child in this family inheriting Huntington's chorea.

....

....

....

....(5)

(Total marks 7)

London

Question 2

The information below is about insulin.

▶ Insulin is a *hormone*, produced by the pancreas, which reduces the concentration of glucose in the blood.

▶ People who cannot produce insulin, or not enough of it, are called diabetics.

▶ Diabetics usually need daily injections of insulin.

▶ For many years this insulin has been extracted from the pancreas of pigs, sheep and cattle.

▶ Scientists can now produce human insulin using a technique known as genetic engineering.

(a) What are *hormones*?

....

....

....(2)

(b) The diagram below shows some of the stages involved in the production of genetically-engineered human insulin.

(i) How is the insulin gene removed from the human chromosome?

....(1)

(ii) The *clone* of bacterium **2** produces large quantites of insulin.

[A] What is a *clone*?

....

....(2)

[B] Explain why bacteria are suitable organisms to use for this purpose.

....

....

....

....(3)

(c) Explain *one* advantage genetically-engineered insulin has compared with that extracted from animals.

....

....(2)

(Total marks 10)
SEG

Question 3

The photograph below shows an Ayrshire cow.
(*In the original examination paper a photograph of an Ayrshire cow was shown.*)

The table shows how the average milk yield per Ayrshire cow increased between 1807 and 1967.

Year	Average yield of milk per cow (litres per year)
1807	1934
1855	2570
1955	3567
1967	4004

(a) Explain, as fully as you can, how farmers might have increased the amount of milk yielded by the cows.

....

....

....

....

....(3)

(b) Give *two* advantages in having cows which produce higher yields of milk.

1. ....

....

2. ....

....(2)

(Total marks 5)
NEAB

Question 4

(a) Domestic animals and cultivated plants can be improved by selective breeding.

(i) Describe the process of selective breeding.

....

....

....

....

....(3)

(ii) State *two* characteristics a farmer could improve in his wheat crop by selective breeding.

....

....

....(2)

(b) Tall, high-yielding tomato plants are deliberately crossed with short, disease-resistant tomato plants.

The genotype of the tall plant is HH and that of the short plant is hh. The dominant allele is H.

(i) Write the genotype of the F_1 generation plants.

....(1)

(ii) What proportion of the F_1 generation plants would be tall?

....(1)

(iii) The F_1 generation plants are allowed to self-pollinate. The seeds from this cross are grown.

State and explain the probable proportions of tall and short plants in the offspring.

....

....

....

....(2)

(c) Genetic engineers can be successful in changing characteristics of some plants and animals. Scientists are trying to transfer the nitrogen-fixing ability associated with plants such as peas into crops such as cereals.

(i) Describe how the characteristics of an organism can be changed by genetic engineering.

....

....

....

....(3)

(ii) In developing new varieties of plants by genetic engineering, what danger should scientists be aware of and what precautions should they take?

....

....

....

....

....(3)

(Total marks 15)

MEG

4 Ecology

Ecology is the study of the relationships between the **living factors** (animals and plants) and **non-living factors** (climate; soil; circulation of carbon, nitrogen and water) in the environment. Together these living and non-living factors make up the basic unit in ecology, the **ecosystem**.

1 Population, competition and adaptation

To survive in the natural world, organisms (animals and plants) must compete with each other for **resources**. In an overpopulated environment where resources are in short supply, organisms need to compete with each other so that they can survive long enough to breed and reproduce.

Population

Population is the number of any one species in a particular area. Population size is controlled by:

1 **competition** for food, water and space between members of the same species (this also affects the distribution of a population);
2 **predation** – an increase in the number of predators reduces the number of prey; an increase in the number of prey increases the number of predators, as shown by the graph;

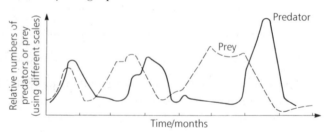

Figure 4.1
The population of the prey affects the numbers of the predator

3 **migration** – animals migrating into or out of an area increases or decreases the size of the population of that species.

Adaptation

Adaptation refers to the development of special features which enable an animal or plant to live in a particular environment.

▶ *Animal adaptations* may include the amount of body fat and thickness of fur, size of body and surface area: for example, polar bears are adapted to live in the cold climate of the arctic, camels are adapted to live in the dry arid desert areas. Predators are usually well adapted to catch their prey but the prey animals are well adapted, e.g. by camouflage, to escape!
▶ *Plant adaptations* may include waxy cuticle and reduced size of leaves to reduce water loss by transpiration.

2 Energy and nutrient transfer

Some key words you need to know about ecosystems:

▶ A **food chain** shows how an animal obtains its **energy** (food) from another animal or plant; the arrows show the direction of **energy transfer** between the trophic levels.

▶ A **food web** shows how an animal may be obtaining energy from more than one source, or how a plant may be supplying energy to several different organisms.

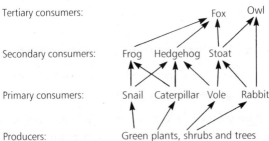

Figure 4.2
In a food web one animal feeds on more than source of food

▶ **Producers** are green plants making their own food by **photosynthesis** at the first trophic level of a food web.
▶ **Primary consumers (herbivores)** obtain energy directly from producers (green plants); primary consumers are on the second trophic level of a food web.
▶ **Secondary consumers (carnivores)** obtain energy from primary consumers (herbivores); they are at the third trophic level.
▶ **Tertiary consumers (carnivores)** obtain energy from other consumers in the food web.
▶ A **pyramid of numbers** shows the number of organisms at each level of a food chain; for example there are usually more producers than consumers.

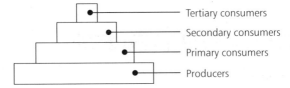

Figure 4.3
Pyramid of numbers

▶ A **pyramid of biomass** shows the mass of organisms at each level of a food chain; for example the biomass of the producers is greater than the biomass of consumers.
Ⓗ ▶ Energy is lost at each trophic level; for example, a cow loses 60% of the available energy through excretion and about 30% through respiration and movement, so only about 10% of the available energy is transferred from the cow to humans.

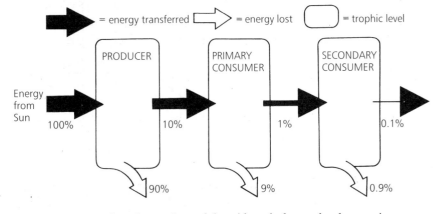

Figure 4.4
Energy is lost at each stage of the food chain

HINT
You do not have to draw the cycles from memory but only complete diagrams provided in the question, so make sure you look at nitrogen and carbon cycles in your notes, and practise filling in the boxes!

▶ **Decomposers** such as bacteria and fungi break down dead organic matter (dead animals and plants) and release **nutrients** into the soil for recycling, such as carbon and nitrogen.
▶ The key stages of the **carbon cycle** are:

carbon dioxide in air ⟶ photosynthesis ⟶ respiration and combustion

▶ The key stages of the **nitrogen cycle** are:

nitrogen in air ⟶ fixed as plant protein ⟶ animal protein ⟶
death and decay ⟶ ammonia ⟶ nitrates

3 Impact of human activity on the environment

Rapid increase in the world population has caused environmental problems, such as **pollution** of air, water and land.

▶ Burning **fossil fuels** releases waste gases, including large amounts of **carbon dioxide** which contribute to the **greenhouse effect**: heat is absorbed by carbon dioxide (and methane) in the atmosphere and radiated back to Earth, causing **global warming**, melting of ice caps in polar regions and an increase in sea level leading to flooding of coastal regions.

▶ **CFCs** (chlorofluorocarbons) used as propellants for aerosols and as refrigerants cause breakdown of the **ozone layer** which absorbs harmful UV rays from Sun, leading to a rise in skin cancer (melanoma).

▶ **Deforestation** (removal of large areas of trees), together with removal of ground vegetation and overgrazing, exposes the soil to wind and water, leading to **erosion** of topsoil and **desertification** (land changes into a desert); the land then produces less food and sustains fewer livestock. Desertification affects up to 20% of world population.

PRACTICE QUESTIONS

Question 1

Some rabbits were released on an island. There were no predators of rabbits on the island. The graph shows changes in the size of the rabbit population over a number of years.

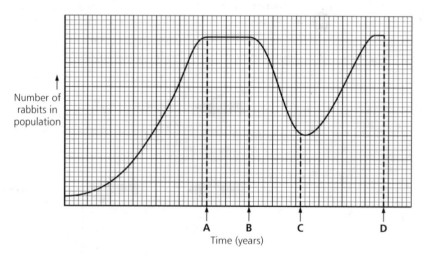

(a) (i)   What has happened to the rabbit population at **A**?

....

....(1)

(ii) Suggest why this has happened.

....

....(2)

(b) (i) At **B**, a few predators of the rabbits arrived on the island.
Suggest why the rabbit population falls between **B** and **C**.

....

....

....(1)

(ii) Explain what will happen to the predator population between **B** and **C**.

....

....

....

....(2)

(iii) Explain what is likely to happen to the numbers of rabbits and
predators over the years following **D**.

....

....

....

....

....(3)

(Total marks 9)
London

Question 2
The diagram below shows a food web for a wood.

(a) Construct a food chain which contains *four* organisms including shrews.

(2)

(b) Explain what would happen to the populations of small birds and moths if the
gamekeeper succeeds in catching some of the weasels.

....

....

....

....(4)

(c) The diagrams below show a pyramid of numbers and a pyramid of biomass for 0.1 hectare of this wood.

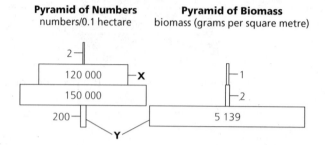

Pyramid of Numbers
numbers/0.1 hectare

Pyramid of Biomass
biomass (grams per square metre)

(i) Name *one* organism from the level labelled **X**.

....(1)

(ii) Explain, as fully as you can, why the level labelled **Y** is such a different width in the two pyramids.

....

....

....

....(3)

(d) A 1 m² area of the floor of the wood was fenced off so that animals could not reach it. The graph shows the depth of leaf litter inside the fenced area over the next few months.

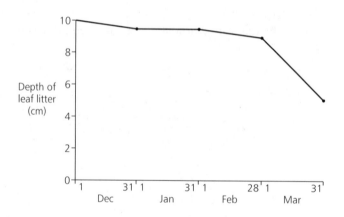

(i) Explain, as fully as you can, why and how the leaf litter gradually disappeared.

....

....

....

....(2)

(ii) In which month does leaf litter disappear fastest? Explain why.

....

....

....

....(2)

(iii) Explain, as fully as you can, how nitrogen from the protein molecules in the leaf litter eventually becomes part of the protein molecules of new leaves.

....

....

....

....

....

....(6)

(Total marks 20)
NEAB

Question 3

(a) The diagram *(below)* shows what happens to 1 000 000 kJ of the Sun's energy falling on a field of grass grazed by a cow.

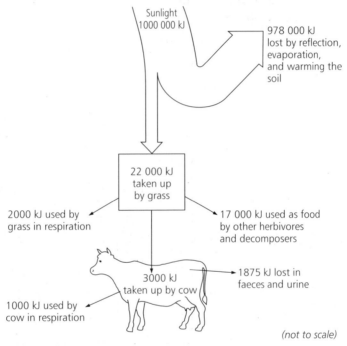

(not to scale)

(i)   Of the 1 000 000 kJ of sunlight energy falling on the field of grass grazed by a cow, calculate the percentage which is retained by the cow for growth. Show your working.

....

....(2)

(ii) Use the information in the diagram to explain why it is more energy efficient for humans to eat plants rather than animals.

....

....

....(2)

(b) Some of the energy lost from cattle is present in methane gas. Methane is a 'greenhouse gas'. These gases in the atmosphere trap energy. The greater the concentration of greenhouse gases there is in the atmosphere, the more global warming will occur. This is called the 'greenhouse effect'.

(i) Explain how the greenhouse effect leads to global warming.
     A diagram may help to make your answer clear.

     ....

     ....

     ....

     ....(4)

(ii) Explain why an increase in greenhouse gases in the atmosphere could
     cause major changes to the environment on Earth.

     ....

     ....

     ....(3)

                                                                    (Total marks 11)
                                                                          MEG

Question 4

The graph shows changes in the estimated size of the world population since
1700.

(a) The world population doubled between 1750 and 1900, a total of 150 years.
    How long did it take for the population to double from the size it was in 1950?

....(1)

(b) Discuss the environmental problems which are likely to occur if the current
    rate of increase of the population continues.

    ....

    ....

    ....

    ....

    ....(6)

                                                                    (Total marks 7)
                                                                          London

Question 5

The diagram shows part of the carbon cycle.

(a) Using the best words from the following list, complete boxes 1, 2, 3, 4 and 5 in the diagram.

burning   decomposition   feeding

photosynthesis   respiration   transpiration

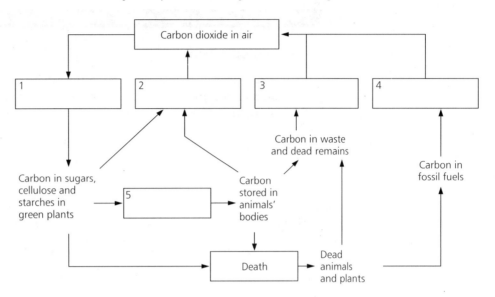

(b) (i) Why is decomposition important in an ecosystem?

....

....

....(2)

(ii) Name *two* types of organisms that are important in decomposition.

....

....(2)

(Total marks 9)

MEG

5 The periodic table, atomic structure and bonding

TOPIC OUTLINE AND REVISION TIPS

1 The periodic table

This is a chart showing all the elements arranged in order of increasing **atomic number** (the lightest atoms are at the top left and the heaviest at the bottom right).

Figure 5.1
The periodic table

					1 **H** Hydrogen 1												4 **He** Helium 2
7 **Li** Lithium 3	9 **Be** Beryllium 4											11 **B** Boron 5	12 **C** Carbon 6	14 **N** Nitrogen 7	16 **O** Oxygen 8	19 **F** Fluorine 9	20 **Ne** Neon 10
23 **Na** Sodium 11	24 **Mg** Magnesium 12											27 **Al** Aluminium 13	28 **Si** Silicon 14	31 **P** Phosphorus 15	32 **S** Sulphur 16	35.5 **Cl** Chlorine 17	40 **Ar** Argon 18
39 **K** Potassium 19	40 **Ca** Calcium 20	45 **Sc** Scandium 21	48 **Ti** Titanium 22	51 **V** Vanadium 23	52 **Cr** Chromium 24	55 **Mn** Manganese 25	56 **Fe** Iron 26	59 **Co** Cobalt 27	59 **Ni** Nickel 28	64 **Cu** Copper 29	65 **Zn** Zinc 30	70 **Ga** Gallium 31	73 **Ge** Germanium 32	75 **As** Arsenic 33	79 **Se** Selenium 34	80 **Br** Bromine 35	84 **Kr** Krypton 36
85 **Rb** Rubidium 37	88 **Sr** Strontium 38	89 **Y** Yttrium 39	91 **Zr** Zirconium 40	93 **Nb** Niobium 41	96 **Mo** Molybdenum 42	**Tc** Technetium 43	101 **Ru** Ruthenium 44	103 **Rh** Rhodium 45	106 **Pd** Palladium 46	108 **Ag** Silver 47	112 **Cd** Cadmium 48	115 **In** Indium 49	119 **Sn** Tin 50	122 **Sb** Antimony 51	128 **Te** Tellurium 52	127 **I** Iodine 53	131 **Xe** Xenon 54
133 **Cs** Caesium 55	137 **Ba** Barium 56	139 **La** Lanthanum 57	178 **Hf** Hafnium 72	181 **Ta** Tantalum 73	184 **W** Tungsten 74	186 **Re** Rhenium 75	190 **Os** Osmium 76	192 **Ir** Iridium 77	195 **Pt** Platinum 78	197 **Au** Gold 79	201 **Hg** Mercury 80	204 **Tl** Thallium 81	207 **Pb** Lead 82	209 **Bi** Bismuth 83	**Po** Polonium 84	**At** Astatine 85	**Rn** Radon 86
Fr Francium 87	226 **Ra** Radium 88	227 **Ac** Actinium 89 †															

← **Metals** → ← **Non-Metals** →

- A **period** is a horizontal row of elements (going across) showing these *general trends*:
  - elements change from metals to non-metals;
  - the number of electrons in the outer shell increases from 1 to 8 (the number of electrons in the outer shell is equal to the **group number**);
  - the **valency** of elements increases from 1 to 4 in groups 1 to 4, then decreases from 4 to 1 in groups 4 to 7;
  - melting points and boiling points of elements increase to a maximum for group 4 then decrease again to group 0.

Figure 5.2
Trends across the 3rd period

Metal/non-metal	***Na*** ***m***	***Mg*** ***m***	***Al*** ***m***	***Si*** ***n/m***	***P*** ***n/m***	***S*** ***n/m***	***Cl*** ***n/m***	***Ar*** ***n/m***
Outer shell electrons	1	2	3	4	5	6	7	8
Valency	1	2	3	4	3	2	1	0
Oxidation no.	+1	+2	+3	+4	−3	−2	−1	0
Melting point/°C	98	650	660	1410	44	113	−100	−189
Boiling point/°C	880	1100	2470	2355	280	444	−35	−186
Oxide nature	basic	basic	amphoteric	acidic	acidic	acidic	acidic	–
Formula of oxide	Na_2O	MgO	Al_2O_3	SiO_2	P_2O_3	SO_2	Cl_2O	–
Formula of chloride	$NaCl$	$MgCl_2$	$AlCl_3$	$SiCl_4$	PCl_3	S_2Cl_2	Cl_2	–

- A **group** is a vertical column of elements (going down) showing these *general trends* (gradual change of properties) with increasing atomic number from top to bottom of group:
  - the atoms become larger (their diameter increases);
  - they lose outer electrons more easily;
  - the density of the element increases.

Elements within a group have the same number of electrons in their outer shell (alkali metals, group 1, have one electron in their outer shell) and behave in a similar way in chemical reactions.

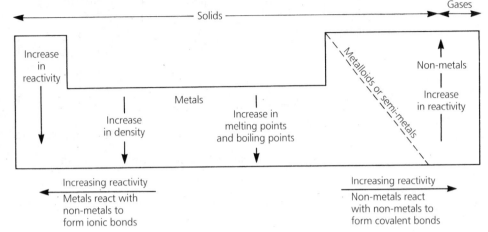

Figure 5.3
Trends in the periodic table. *Remember*, these are general trends – there are exceptions

Properties and reactions of the alkali metals

Group 1 elements – the **alkali metals** – have one electron in their outer shell. The atoms form **ions** with a charge of +1, one electron being removed from the outer shell. Their reactivity increases down the group as the number of shells increases (the further away from the positive nucleus the outer shell is the more easily the electron is lost).

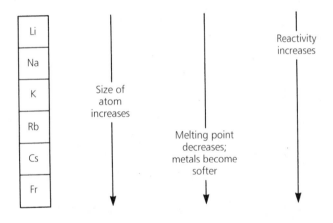

Figure 5.4
The alkali metals

Reactions of the alkali metals lithium, sodium, potassium:

▶ *Reaction with air:* they are very reactive and form **basic oxides** which dissolve in water to form alkaline solutions.

$$4M + O_2 \longrightarrow 2M_2O$$

▶ *Reaction with cold water:* they react quickly to produce strong alkaline **hydroxide** solutions and hydrogen.

$$2M + 2H_2O \longrightarrow 2MOH + H_2$$

▶ *Reaction with halogens:* they react to form **halides**.

$$2M + Cl_2 \longrightarrow 2MCl$$

Properties, reactions and uses of the halogens

Group 7 elements – the **halogens** – have seven electrons in their outer shell. The atoms form ions with a charge of −1, one electron being added to the outer shell. Their reactivity decreases down the group as the number of shells increases (the closer to the pulling power of the positive nucleus the outer shell is the more easily an electron is gained).

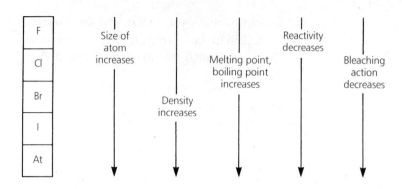

Figure 5.5
The halogens

HINT
Revise the reactions and uses
of the halogens

HINT
Revise the properties, reactions
and uses of simple compounds
of the halogens such as
hydrogen chloride

Reactions of the halogens chlorine, bromine and iodine:

▶ *Reaction with metals:* they form metal halides.

$$3Fe + 3Cl_2 \longrightarrow 2FeCl_3$$

▶ *Reaction with water:* they form acidic solutions which act as **bleaches**.

$$H_2O + Cl_2 \longrightarrow HOCl \text{ (chloric acid)}$$

Remember that chlorine is used as a *bleaching agent* and for *sterilising* water.

Properties and uses of the noble gases

Group 0 elements – the **noble gases** – have completely filled outer electron shells.

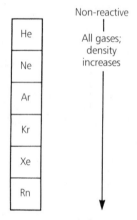

Figure 5.6
The inert gases

▶ Properties of helium, neon and argon: they are colourless and unreactive gases at room temperature.
▶ Uses of noble gases: helium is used for airships, argon in light bulbs, neon in coloured advertising signs.

The transition elements

These are elements between groups 2 and 3 of the table, e.g. iron, manganese, copper, zinc.

HINT
Revise some uses of transition
metals (such as copper wires
and copper pipes)

▶ They are metals with high density and high melting points.
▶ These metals are used as catalysts.

Remember that, due to the colour of the transition metal ion, transition metals form a range of brightly coloured compounds.

2 Atomic structure

Solids, liquids and gases are all composed of particles. Adding energy by heating can cause a **change of state** from a solid to a liquid to a gas; the reverse occurs by removing energy during cooling.

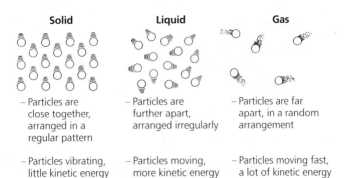

Solid	Liquid	Gas
– Particles are close together, arranged in a regular pattern	– Particles are further apart, arranged irregularly	– Particles are far apart, in a random arrangement
– Particles vibrating, little kinetic energy	– Particles moving, more kinetic energy	– Particles moving fast, a lot of kinetic energy

Figure 5.7

Structure of atoms

Atoms have a central **nucleus** containing positively charged **protons** and neutral **neutrons**, surrounded by a cloud of negatively charged **electrons** arranged in shells.

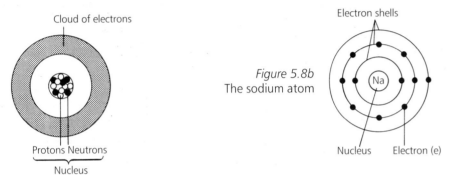

Figure 5.8a
Particles which make up the atom

Cloud of electrons

Protons Neutrons

Nucleus

Electron shells

Figure 5.8b
The sodium atom

Na

Nucleus   Electron (e)

Subatomic particle	Relative mass	Relative charge
Proton	1	+1
Neutron	1	0
Electron	very small	−1

▶ The **mass number** (Z) (or nucleon number) is the number of protons + the number of neutrons in the atomic nucleus.

▶ The **atomic number** (A) is the number of protons in the nucleus (= the number of electrons).

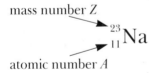

mass number Z

$$^{23}_{11}\text{Na}$$

atomic number A

▶ **Isotopes** are atoms of same element which contain *different numbers of neutrons* (but same number of protons) and so have *different mass numbers*: for example, chlorine has two istotopes Cl-35 (18 neutrons) and Cl-37 (20 neutrons); there are three Cl-35 for every one Cl-37 in chlorine gas, so the average number of protons and neutrons in the nucleus is 35.5.

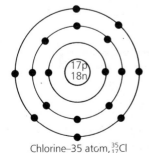

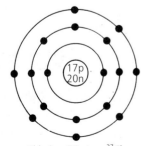

Figure 5.9
Isotopes of chlorine

Chlorine–35 atom, $^{35}_{17}\text{Cl}$

Chlorine–37 atom, $^{37}_{17}\text{Cl}$

3 Bonding

▶ **Compounds** are new substances formed when *more than one type of atom* become chemically combined: for example, sodium chloride consists of sodium ions and chlorine ions; it can be split by electrolysis into sodium atoms and chlorine atoms.

▶ Atoms react together to fill the outer electron shell and become stable.

There are two types of chemical bonding: **ionic** and **covalent**.

▶ In **ionic bonding** atoms *lose or gain electrons* (by transfer of electrons): for example in forming sodium chloride the sodium atom loses an electron to become a positively charged sodium ion (Na^+); the chlorine atom gains an electron to become a negatively charged chlorine ion (Cl^-). The ions have both filled their outer shells and attract each other electrostatically due to opposite charges.

Remember:

ions are formed when atoms gain or lose electrons; metals form positive ions (**cations**) by losing electrons; non-metals form negative ions (**anions**) by gaining electrons; ionic lattices are held together by attraction between oppositely charged ions.

Figure 5.10
Formation of ions when sodium reacts with chlorine

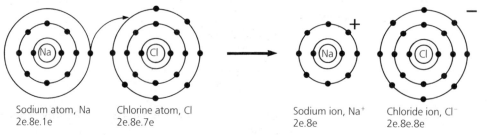

Sodium atom, Na
2e.8e.1e

Chlorine atom, Cl
2e.8e.7e

Sodium ion, Na⁺
2e.8e

Chloride ion, Cl⁻
2e.8e.8e

H ▶ In **covalent bonding** atoms *share pairs of electrons* in their outer shells: for example, non-metal atoms such as hydrogen form molecules by sharing electrons.

Figure 5.11
Covalent bonding

or H − H

The hydrogen molecule

or O = O

The oxygen molecule

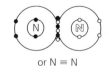

or N ≡ N

The nitrogen molecule

The table shows the differences in properties of ionic and covalent compounds.

	Ionic compounds	*Covalent compounds*
Relation to periodic table	Formed between metal atoms and non-metal atoms	Formed between non-metal atoms
Melting point	High >250°C	Low <250°C
Boiling point	High >500°C	Low <500°C
Electrical conductivity	Good conductor when molten or in solution	Non-conductors
Solubility in water	Usually soluble	Usually insoluble

PRACTICE QUESTIONS

Question 1

Use your periodic table and your knowledge of more familiar elements to *suggest* answers to the following questions. You are not expected to *know* about the chemistry of rubidium, iodine and selenium.

(a) Rubidium, Rb, has the atomic number 37.

(i) In what group of the periodic table is rubidium?

....(1)

(ii) Name the *two* products you would expect when rubidium reacts with water.

....

and...(2)

(iii) Suggest *two* observations which you might *see* during the reaction.

....

and...(2)

(b) Iodine, I, has the atomic number 53. It reacts with hydrogen to form a gas, hydrogen iodide.

$$H_2 + I_2 \longrightarrow 2HI$$

Hydrogen iodide is very soluble in water.

(i) Name a common laboratory liquid you would expect to behave like hydrogen iodide solution.

....(1)

(ii) What *two* products would you expect to be formed when magnesium reacts with hydrogen iodide solution?

....

and...(2)

(iii) Suggest *two* observations which you might *see* during the reaction.

....

and...(2)

(c) Selenium, Se, has the atomic number 34. Selenium trioxide reacts with water to form a new compound.

$$H_2O(l) + SeO_2(s) \longrightarrow H_2SeO_4(aq)$$

(i) What effect would the solution have on Universal indicator (full-range indicator)?

....(1)

(ii) Suggest *two* observations you might *see* when this solution was added to sodium carbonate.

....

and...(2)

(iii) Name one of the compounds formed in the reaction with sodium carbonate.

....(1)

(Total marks 14)
London

HINT

You may want to revise electrolysis (Chapter 6, p. 49) before trying this question

Question 2

This question is about sodium chloride (common salt) which is an important chemical.

Sodium chloride can be made by burning sodium in chlorine gas.
(In the original examination paper a photograph of the burning reaction was shown.)

(a) Balance the equation for the reaction of sodium with chlorine.

$$......Na + Cl_2 \longrightarrow ......NaCl$$ (1)

(b) (i) Complete the diagrams to show the electronic structure of a sodium atom and a chlorine atom.

Sodium atom   Chlorine atom

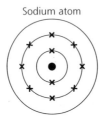   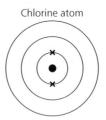

(2)

   (ii) How does a sodium atom change into a sodium ion?

....

....(2)

(c) The apparatus shown can be used to electrolyse sodium chloride solution.

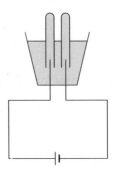

   (i) Name the product formed at:

   1. the positive electrode...

   2. the negative electrode ....(2)

   (ii) Give *one* large-scale use of the product formed at the negative electrode.

....(1)

   (iii) The final solution contains Na^+ ions and OH^- ions.
        Name the useful chemical that could be obtained from this solution.

....(1)

(d) The element potassium is in the same group of the periodic table as sodium. Potassium reacts with chlorine to make potassium chloride. This is sometimes used in cooking instead of common salt.

   (i) Give the chemical formula of potassium chloride. ....(1)

(ii) By reference to the electronic structures of sodium and potassium, explain why the reaction of sodium with chlorine is similar to the reaction of potassium with chlorine.

....

....(1)

(e) Fluorine is the most reactive element in group 7 of the periodic table. It reacts with all the other elements in the periodic table except some of the noble gases. It does not react with helium, argon and neon, but it does react with xenon (Xe) to form xenon fluoride.

(i) Explain why fluorine is more reactive than chlorine.

....

....

....(3)

(ii) Explain why the noble gases are generally unreactive.

....

....

....(3)

(iii) Predict, with reasons, whether radon (Rn) will react with fluorine.

....

....

....

....(3)

(Total marks 20)

NEAB

HINT

You may want to revise radioactivity (Chapter 13, p. 101) before trying this question.

Question 3

(a) Carbon dating is used to check the age of dead animal or plant material. The carbon in living things is mainly carbon–12, but there is also a small amount of carbon–14. Carbon–14 is a radioactive isotope.

(i) Complete the atomic structure of carbon–14. Carbon–12 has been completed for you.

Carbon–12   Carbon–14   (3)

(ii) Name the particles represented by $\oplus$, ● and $\ominus$.

$\oplus$.............................   ●............................. $\ominus$.........................   (3)

(iii) What does *radioactive* mean?

....

....

....(2)

(iv) What does *isotope* mean?

....

....

....

....(3)

(b) Graphite and diamond are two different forms of carbon. Graphite and diamond have different structures and uses.

Diamond

Graphite

Use the idea of molecular structures to answer these questions.

(i) Why is diamond a very hard substance?

....

....

....(2)

(ii) Why is graphite a soft, slippery substance?

....

....

....(2)

(iii) Why do both diamond and graphite have very high melting points?

....

....(1)

(c) The diagram shows an electric cell. The negative electrode is made from zinc.

Carbon (positive)
electrode

Zinc (negative)
electrode

Which form of carbon would be used for the positive electrode? Explain why.

....

....

....(2)

(d) Both the metal zinc and the non-metal carbon form oxides.

   (i) Give one *physical* difference between a typical metal oxide and a non-metal oxide.

   ....(1)

   (ii) Give one *chemical* difference between a typical metal oxide and a non-metal oxide.

   ....(1)

(Total marks 20)

SEG

Question 4

The diagram below shows the first three rows of the periodic table.

KEY
Atomic number

Relative atomic mass

1
X
1

1							2
H							**He**
Hydrogen							Helium
1							4
3	4	5	6	7	8	9	10
Li	**Be**	**B**	**C**	**N**	**O**	**F**	**Ne**
Lithium	Beryllium	Boron	Carbon	Nitrogen	Oxygen	Fluorine	Neon
7	9	11	12	14	16	19	20
11	12	13	14	15	16	17	18
Na	**Mg**	**Al**	**Si**	**P**	**S**	**Cl**	**Ar**
Sodium	Magnesium	Aluminium	Silicon	Phosphorus	Sulphur	Chlorine	Argon
23	24	27	28	31	32	35.5	40

(a) Describe and explain the pattern in the electronic structures of these 18 elements.

   ....

   ....

   ....

   ....

   ....

   ....(3)

(b) Explain why the charge on a sodium ion is +1 but the charge on a chloride ion is −1.

   ....

   ....

   ....(2)

(Total marks 5)

London

Useful products from oil and metals

6

TOPIC OUTLINE AND REVISION TIPS

1 Useful products from oil

Crude oil (petroleum) and natural gas (methane) are formed by the effects of heat and pressure on organic matter trapped in sediments. They are mixtures of **hydrocarbons**: compounds of carbon and hydrogen only.

Separation into fractions

Fractional distillation is used to separate crude oil into different **fractions** (mixtures of hydrocarbons with similar boiling points); products such as petrol, paraffin, diesel oil are used as **fuels**.

▶ Smaller hydrocarbon molecules (liquid gas, petrol, paraffin) have lower boiling points, are very flammable and very volatile.
▶ Larger hydrocarbon molecules (fuel oil, grease, bitumen) have higher boiling points, burn with smoky flames and are less volatile.

Combustion

▶ **Complete combustion** is an **exothermic** reaction, occurring when there is a plentiful supply of oxygen:

$$\text{fuel (methane)} + \text{oxygen} \longrightarrow \text{carbon dioxide} + \text{water} + \text{energy (heat)}$$
$$CH_4 + 2O_2 \longrightarrow CO_2 + 2H_2O + \text{energy (heat)}$$

▶ **Incomplete combustion** occurs when fuel burns in a limited amount of oxygen; poisonous carbon monoxide is formed.
▶ **Pollutants** such as carbon, carbon monoxide, sulphur dioxide and oxides of nitrogen can be formed during combustion.

Alkanes and alkenes

Figure 6.1
Structural formula of
ethane C_2H_6

▶ **Alkanes** are **saturated** hydrocarbon molecules, having single covalent bonds between two carbon atoms C—C, e.g. methane CH_4, ethane C_2H_6, propane C_3H_8, butane C_4H_{10}.
▶ **Cracking** is thermal decomposition using a catalyst, to break down long hydrocarbon molecules into shorter more useful chains; alkanes are cracked to form alkenes, e.g. ethene.
▶ **Alkenes** are **unsaturated** hydrocarbon molecules, having double covalent bonds between two carbon atoms C=C, e.g. ethene C_2H_4, propene C_3H_6.
▶ **Polymers** are large molecules which can be formed by combining many small molecules: for example, unsaturated monomers (alkenes such as ethene) formed during cracking are made into **addition polymers** (such as poly(ethene) used for plastic bags and bottles).

Figure 6.2
Structural formula of
ethene C_2H_4

Remember a test to distinguish between alkanes and alkenes: a colourless solution is formed when an alkene is shaken with bromine water; alkanes only decolourise bromine water very slowly.

2 Useful products from metal ores and rocks

Metal **ores** are rocks containing **minerals** (metal compounds) or metals. **Extraction** (separation) of the metal from its ore depends on its **reactivity**; the more reactive metals have more stable compounds and more energy is required to reduce the metal ion to the metal atom.

The reactivity series for metals

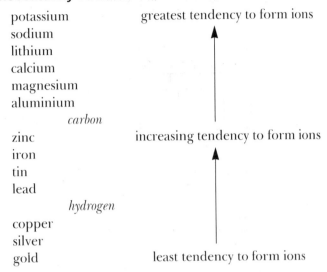

potassium — greatest tendency to form ions
sodium
lithium
calcium
magnesium
aluminium
     carbon
zinc — increasing tendency to form ions
iron
tin
lead
    hydrogen
copper
silver
gold — least tendency to form ions

The reactivity series can help us understand:

► why some metals corrode and not others
► how we can prevent corrosion
► why some metals react with dilute acids and not others
► why some metals are extracted from their ores by reduction with carbon and why some can only be extracted by electrolysis
► why metals were discovered in the order they were

Extraction techniques

There are two basic extraction techniques: **electrolysis** and **reduction** by carbon or carbon monoxide.

Extraction by electrolysis

► Electrolysis involves the passing of an electric current through a molten or dissolved **electrolyte**. Negatively charged ions (**anions**) flow to the positive terminal (**anode**) and positively charged ions (**cations**) flow to the negative terminal (**cathode**).

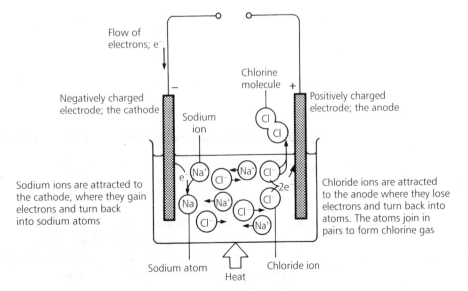

Figure 6.3
Electrolysis of molten sodium chloride

Flow of electrons; e⁻

Chlorine molecule

Negatively charged electrode; the cathode

Sodium ion

Positively charged electrode; the anode

Sodium ions are attracted to the cathode, where they gain electrons and turn back into sodium atoms

Chloride ions are attracted to the anode where they lose electrons and turn back into atoms. The atoms join in pairs to form chlorine gas

Sodium atom

Heat

Chloride ion

▶ Extraction by electrolysis is used for more reactive metals such as aluminium; it can be expensive as large amounts of energy are required.

Aluminium is extracted from bauxite (mainly aluminium oxide). The ore is first concentrated by removing the impurities; because of its high melting point (about 2000°C) the concentrate ('alumina') is then dissolved in molten cryolite at 1000°C: the solution formed has free aluminium ions, which change into atoms at the cathode and the metal is run off.

Figure 6.4
Extraction of aluminium by electrolysis of alumina

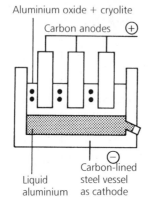

HINT

Look up in your notes the purification of copper by electrolysis of copper sulphate solution

Reduction by carbon

▶ Reduction with carbon is used for less reactive metals: for example, the reduction of iron ore to iron; raw materials are coke (a cheap source of carbon), haematite (iron oxide), limestone and air.

Figure 6.5
The blast furnace used to extract iron from iron ore

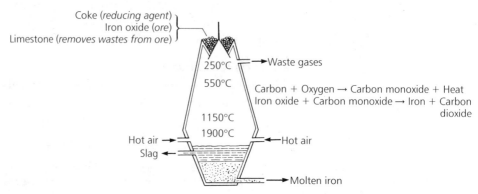

$$\text{carbon} + \text{oxygen} \longrightarrow \text{carbon monoxide}$$
$$2C(s) + O_2(g) \longrightarrow 2CO(g)$$

$$\text{carbon monoxide} + \text{iron oxide} \longrightarrow \text{iron} + \text{carbon dioxide}$$
$$3CO(g) + Fe_2O_3(s) \longrightarrow 2Fe(l) + 3CO_2(g)$$

3 Problems associated with oil and metal usage

The constant demand for raw materials can produce problems:

▶ *social:* the creation of jobs and towns may be due to the location of a particular raw material, e.g. coal, gold, which may run out;
▶ *environmental:* pollution from waste materials, e.g. slag heaps; destruction of the environment, e.g. mining and quarrying;
▶ *economic:* a country's economy may be based on the fluctuating price of one raw material such as copper or uranium.

PRACTICE QUESTIONS

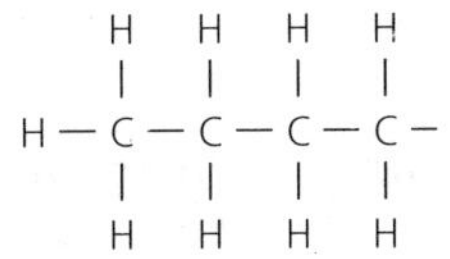

```
  H   H   H   H
  |   |   |   |
H─C ─ C ─ C ─ C ─
  |   |   |   |
  H   H   H   H
```
Figure 6.6

Question 1
Crude oil is a mixture of many compounds. Most of these compounds are hydrocarbons. The structure of one of these compounds is shown in the diagram.

(a) What is a hydrocarbon?

....(1)

(b) What is the chemical formula of the structure shown in the diagram?

....(1)

(c) Crude oil consists of a large number of different compounds. Fractional distillation and cracking can be used to produce useful compounds from crude oil.

Describe, in as much details as you can, how these two processes produce alkanes that are useful as fuels.

....

....

....

....

....(5)

(d) Ethene is an unsaturated hydrocarbon. What is meant by the term 'unsaturated'?

....(1)

(e) Complete the following equation to show how three ethene molecules join together to form part of a poly(ethene) molecule.

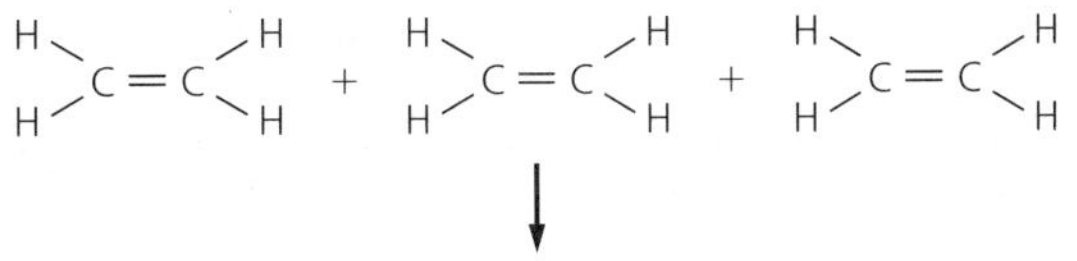

(2)

(f) (i) Suggest one property of poly(ethene) which makes it suitable as a material for food containers.

....(1)

(ii) Thermosetting plastics cannot be re-moulded after they have been heated and allowed to cool. Explain why.

....

....

....(2)

(Total marks 13)
NEAB

Question 2

(a) The table below gives some information about the group of hydrocarbons called the alkanes.

Name	Formula	Melting point (°C)	Boiling point (°C)	Density (g/cm³)	Energy released by combustion (kJ/mol)
Methane	CH_4	−182	−162	0.53	890
Ethane	C_2H_6	−183	−89	0.55	1560
Propane	C_3H_8	−188	−42	0.57	2220
Butane	C_4H_{10}	−138	−1	____	2880
Pentane	C_5H_{12}	−130	+36	0.63	____
Hexane		−95	+69	0.66	4200

(i) What is the pattern linking density and the amount of heat energy released by combustion?

....

....(1)

(ii) Suggest a value for the density of butane.

....(1)

(iii) What pattern is shown by the formulae of the alkanes?

....

....(2)

(iv) Use the pattern to predict the formula of hexane.

....(1)

(b) The graph (*opposite*) shows how the energy released by combustion (y axis) changes with the number of carbon atoms (x axis) for the alkanes.

(i) Use the graph to estimate the energy released by combustion of pentane.

....(1)

(ii) What part of the air is needed for the pentane to burn?

....(1)

(iii) What *two* substances are formed when pentane is burnt in a good supply of air?

.... and...(2)

(iv) Name another substance that is formed when pentane is burnt in a limited supply of air.

....(1)

(v) The flame formed when hydrocarbons are burned becomes smokier as the number of carbon atoms increases. Suggest a reason why.

....

....(1)

(Total marks 11)
London

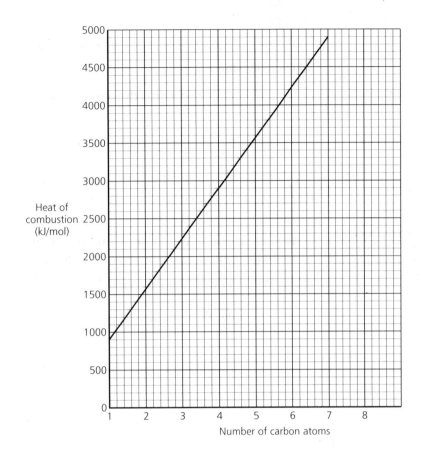

Question 3

Aluminium is extracted from aluminium oxide (Al_2O_3) by electrolysis.
Aluminium oxide contains Al^{3+} and O^{2-} ions. For the electrolysis, aluminium
oxide is dissolved in molten cryolite.

(a) Why can the electrolysis *not* be carried out on *solid* aluminium oxide?

....

....(1)

(b) Aluminium is collected at the cathode. Explain how this happens and write an
ionic equation for the process.

....

....

....

....(2)

Ionic equation: ....(1)

(c) Explain why the carbon *anode* has to be replaced regularly.

....

....

....

....(2)

(Total marks 6)

London

Question 4

A miner in a gold mine uses a steel axe to dig out gold from the rock.

(a) Complete these sentences.

(i) Gold can be taken directly from the rock because

....(1)

(ii) The axe is made from steel because

....(1)

(b) Iron is made from iron ore using a blast furnace. The diagram shows a blast furnace.

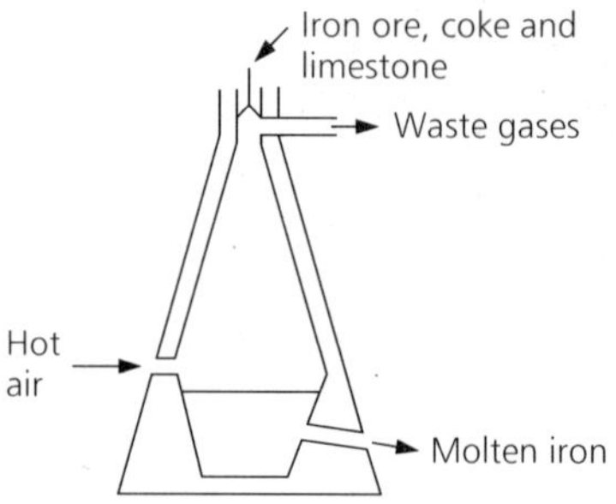

Iron ore contains iron oxide. To make iron, the oxygen has to be separated from the iron. The carbon in coke can do this.

Iron ore, coke and limestone

Waste gases

Hot air

Molten iron

Figure 6.9

(i) Which word below describes changing iron oxide into iron?

| Melting, Rusting, Electrolysis, Reduction, Oxidation |

....(1)

Explain your choice.

....

....(1)

(ii) Use some of these words to write a word equation for a reaction making iron inside the furnace.

| Iron, Limestone, Carbon Dioxide, Iron Oxide, Carbon, Air |

.... + ... ⟶ .... + ...(2)

(iii) Hot air is blown into the furnace. What does this do to the coke inside?

....

....

....(2)

(c) The price of 1 kg of each of the three metals is shown in the table below.

Metal	Price of 1 kg
Gold	£8500
Aluminium	120p
Iron	15p

Suggest reasons why the prices of the metals are so different.

....

....

....

....(3)

(Total marks 11)

London

Chemical reactions

TOPIC OUTLINE AND REVISION TIPS

1 Representing reactions

A chemical reaction is a rearrangement of the atoms in the **reactant(s)** to form the atoms of **product(s)**:

reactant(s) $\longrightarrow$ product(s)

An energy change sometimes occurs, detected by a change in temperature. The products will have different properties from the reactants.

H ▶ The total number of atoms on the left side = the total number of atoms on the right side.

H ▶ The total mass of the reactants = the total mass of the products.

▶ Balanced symbolic equations use the chemical symbols (see the periodic table, p. 42) and show the number of atoms:

$2Na + Cl_2 \longrightarrow 2NaCl$

H The formula for sodium chloride is NaCl, the chlorine molecule has 2 atoms so if there are 2Cl on the left there must be 2Cl on the right, and 2Na on the left to balance.

> **HINT**
> Count the atoms in this reaction:
> $2NaOH + H_2SO_4 \longrightarrow Na_2 + 2H_2O$
> Look in your notes for more examples of balanced equations

▶ The **state** of the reactants and products is shown in equations by state symbols: (g) gas; (l) liquid; (s) solid; (aq) aqueous state (dissolved in water).

$Mg(s) + 2HCl(aq) \longrightarrow MgCl_2(aq) + H_2(g)$

H ▶ **Ionic equations** show the ions involved in a reaction (and ignore the ions that are unchanged); for example,
in neutralisation: $OH^-(aq) + H^+(aq) \longrightarrow H_2O(l)$
in electrolysis: $2Cl^-(l) + 2e^- \longrightarrow Cl_2(g)$

2 Quantitative chemistry

▶ Atoms of different elements have different masses; to work out what is happening in reactions you need to know the **relative atomic masses** (A_r).

▶ The **mole** is the amount of substance that contains the same number of particles as there are atoms in 12 g of carbon-12, i.e. 6×10^{23}.

$$\text{amount of a substance (mol)} = \frac{\text{mass of substance (g)}}{\text{molar mass (g/mol)}}$$

For example, 12 g of carbon is 1 mol of carbon atoms; 24 g of carbon is 2 mol of carbon atoms; 16 g of oxygen is 1 mol of oxygen atoms.

▶ There are the same number of atoms in 1 mol of atoms of any element, i.e. 6×10^{23}.

▶ The **relative atomic mass** (in atomic mass units) has the same *number* value as the **molar mass** (in grams per mole).

▶ The **molecular mass** contains 1 mol of *molecules*: for example, the mass of 1 mol of water molecules, H_2O, is 18 g ($H_2 = 2$ g, $O = 16$ g).

H ▶ *Calculating the mass of a product formed in a reaction* – for example, to find the mass of magnesium chloride produced when 12 g of magnesium reacts with excess HCl, first write the formula:

$Mg + 2HCl \longrightarrow MgCl_2 + H_2$

HINT

Look in your notes for examples of calculations involving molar solutions

HINT

Look up in your practical notes the results of investigations into factors affecting the reaction between dilute hydrochloric acid and (i) marble chips, (ii) magnesium

This means that 1 mol of Mg (mass 24 g) produces 1 mol of $MgCl_2$ (mass $24 + 35.5 + 35.5 = 95$ g) so 0.5 mol of Mg (mass 12 g) produces 0.5 mol of $MgCl_2$ ($95/2 = 47.5$ g), so a mass of 47.5 g of magnesium chloride is produced in the reaction.

3 Rates of reactions

▶ Reactions vary in speed: for example, rusting is a slow reaction, an explosion is a rapid reaction.

▶ The rate of a reaction can be detected by the *rate of formation of the product*, often a gas, or the *rate of disappearance of reactant*.

▶ The rate of a reaction depends on the frequency of collisions between particles; the rate can be increased by:

1 increasing the *concentration* of a reactant such as an acid: this increases the number of particles present;

2 decreasing the *size of the particles*: this increases the surface area available for reaction (fine particles have a larger total surface area than a lump);

3 increasing the *temperature*: reactions usually proceed more quickly at higher temperatures; more kinetic energy is given to particles which move faster and so the number of collisions per second increases;

4 using a **catalyst**: this speeds up the rate of reaction but is not used up in the reaction; reactants are brought together on the surface of the catalyst. Examples are manganese(IV) oxide in the decomposition of hydrogen peroxide, iron oxide in the manufacture of ammonia.

4 Reactions involving enzymes

Enzymes are **biological catalysts** made up of proteins. Enzymes in yeast convert sugar into alcohol in brewing; other enzymes are used in making cheese and yoghurt. Enzyme-catalysed reactions vary with *pH* and *temperature*: for example, the optimum temperature for fermentation is between 20 and 30°C.

5 Reversible reactions

Some reactions are reversible – they can proceed in both directions; for example, ammonia is manufactured by the **Haber process** in which raw materials, nitrogen (from air) and hydrogen (from natural gas), are combined in the presence of an iron catalyst to produce ammonia, but the ammonia decomposes to produce nitrogen and hydrogen:

$$NH_3 + 3H_2 \Leftrightarrow 2NH_3$$

The **yield** of a reversible reaction depends on conditions: high pressure (200 atmospheres) and high temperature (450°C) favour the production of ammonia in the above reaction.

Figure 7.1
Stages in the production of ammonia

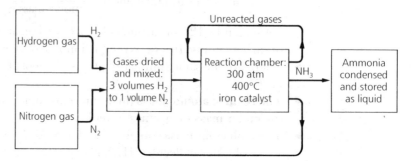

Ammonia can be reacted with oxygen in the presence of a hot platinum catalyst to form nitrogen monoxide, which is then reacted with water to produce nitric acid; nitric acid is neutralised by ammonia to produce ammonia nitrate fertiliser.

6 Energy changes

Energy is needed to break and make bonds.

Endothermic reactions

The breaking of bonds is **endothermic**: heat energy is taken in (for example dissolving potassium chloride in water). In this type of reaction heat is transferred from the surroundings.

Exothermic reactions

The making of bonds is **exothermic**: heat energy is given out (for example, adding a small volume of water to anhydrous copper sulphate). In this type of reaction heat is transferred to the surroundings.

Figure 7.2
Energy level diagrams

Endothermic reaction   Exothermic reaction

PRACTICE QUESTIONS

Question 1

Hydrogen peroxide decomposes very slowly at room temperature.

hydrogen peroxide ⟶ water + oxygen

Adding manganese dioxide speeds up this reaction without altering the products.

A student investigated this reaction by adding 1 g manganese dioxide to 50 cm³ of hydrogen peroxide. The student measured the volume of oxygen produced during five minutes. The results are shown in the table.

Time (minutes)	0	1	2	3	4	5
Total volume of oxygen given off (cm³)	0	27	41	48	50	50

(a) Plot the results (*on a piece of graph paper*). Join the points with a smooth curve. Label your graph 'X'.

(b) The student repeated the experiment. This time the student added 1 g of manganese dioxide to a mixture of 25 cm³ of hydrogen peroxide and 25 cm³ of water.

On your graph, sketch the curve that you would expect if all the other conditions remained the same as in the first experiment.

(c) Explain, in terms of particles, why the rate of the reaction slows down during the experiment.

....

....

....

....(3)

(d) Explain, in terms of particles, why increasing the temperature may increase the rate of a chemical reaction.

....

....

....

....(3)

(e) In a reaction known as 'slaking' water is added to calcium oxide to produce calcium hydroxide. The calcium hydroxide is then used to make plaster.

$$CaO + H_2O \longrightarrow Ca(OH)_2$$

The diagram represents the energy change during this reaction.

CaO + H₂O

Energy change = 65.1 kJ

Ca (OH)₂

(i) What does the diagram tell us about the energy change which takes place in this reaction?

....

....

....(2)

(ii) What does the diagram indicate about the relative amount of energy required to break bonds and form the new bonds in this reaction?

....

....

....

....(3)

(Total marks 17)

NEAB

Question 2

(a) A pupil investigated the electrolysis of water using the apparatus shown. A colourless gas was given off at each electrode.

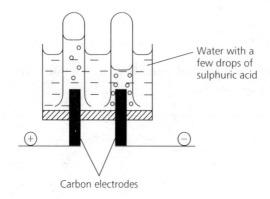

Water with a
few drops of
sulphuric acid

Carbon electrodes

(i) The gas given off at the negative electrode burns with a pop. Name this gas.

....(1)

(ii) The gas given off at the positive electrode relights a glowing splint. Name this gas.

....(1)

(iii) The volume of gas at the negative electrode was twice that at the positive electrode. Explain this.

....

....

....

....(2)

(b) In another experiment the pupil used copper sulphate solution in the electrolysis apparatus. What colour change would the pupil see during the electrolysis?

....

....(1)

(Total marks 5)

SEG

Question 3

This list shows some of the metals in the reactivity series:

zinc (most reactive)
iron
chromium
copper (least reactive)

In its simple chemistry, chromium exists as Cr^{3+} ions, and forms green compounds.

(a) What will you see if an excess of powdered chromium is added to aqueous copper(II) sulphate?

....

....

....

....(2)

(b) Write a balanced symbolic equation for the reaction between chromium and hydrochloric acid.

....(2)

(c) Chromium can be manufactured by the chemical reduction of chromium(III) oxide. Suggest a suitable reagent and the probable conditions for this reduction.

....

....

....

....(1)

(d) Electrolysis is used to coat iron car bumpers with chromium using a suitable solution containing Cr^{3+}.

(i) Predict what will happen to the iron if a chromium plated car bumper is scratched.

....

....(2)

(ii) Complete the ionic equation for the formation of chromium.

Cr^{3+} .... $\longrightarrow$ .... (1)

(Total marks 8)

MEG

Question 4

Ammonia, NH_3, is made by reacting together hydrogen and nitrogen in the presence of iron. This reaction is called the Haber process.

(a) How does the presence of iron help the process?

....(1)

(b) The table shows how much ammonia is produced using different conditions.

Pressure/atm	Percentage yield of ammonia at these temperatures		
	100°C	300°C	500°C
25	91.7	27.4	2.9
50	94.5	39.5	5.6
100	96.7	52.5	10.6
200	98.4	66.7	18.3
400	99.4	79.7	31.9

From the values in the table, what happens to the yield of ammonia as:

(i) the temperature is increased?

....(1)

(ii) the pressure is increased?

....(1)

Using ideas about particles colliding, explain how the rate of the reaction will change as the temperature increases.

....

....

....

....(3)

(d) The Haber process is usually carried out at a higher temperature than the one which would give the highest yield. Suggest a reason for this.

....

....(1)

(Total marks 7)

MEG

8 The solar system; the Earth's geology and atmosphere

TOPIC OUTLINE AND REVISION TIPS

1 The solar system and the wider Universe

The Sun

▶ The Sun is at the centre of our **solar system**; **planets**, **asteroids** (rock debris between Mars and Jupiter) and **comets** orbit the Sun.

▶ The Sun is the source of light and other forms of electromagnetic radiation in our solar system.

▶ The Sun is one of many millions of **stars** which make up the Milky Way **galaxy**, held together by gravitational forces; the **Universe** is a system of many millions of galaxies.

▶ Distances in the Universe are measured in **light years**: one light year is the distance travelled by light in one Earth year.

The planets

▶ The nine planets have elliptical orbits around the Sun due to the **gravitational force of attraction** which exists between the Sun and a planet; orbit time increases the further a planet is from the Sun; the orbits are in the same plane (except that of Pluto).

▶ The planets and the Moon are non-luminous: they *reflect light* from the Sun (stars like the Sun emit their own light).

▶ Most of the planets have natural **satellites** which orbit them, like our Moon.

▶ There are two **groups of planets**:
  – those nearer the Sun (Mercury, Venus, Earth, Mars) have *small diameters* and *high density*;
  – those further from the Sun (Jupiter, Saturn, Uranus, Neptune) have *large diameters* and *low density* (Pluto, the furthest away from the Sun, is an exception – it has a small diameter).

Stars

(H) The life cycle of a star is shown in the diagram.

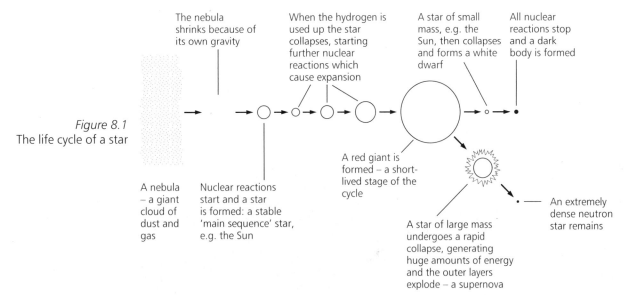

Figure 8.1
The life cycle of a star

The nebula shrinks because of its own gravity

When the hydrogen is used up the star collapses, starting further nuclear reactions which cause expansion

A star of small mass, e.g. the Sun, then collapses and forms a white dwarf

All nuclear reactions stop and a dark body is formed

A red giant is formed – a short-lived stage of the cycle

A nebula – a giant cloud of dust and gas

Nuclear reactions start and a star is formed: a stable 'main sequence' star, e.g. the Sun

A star of large mass undergoes a rapid collapse, generating huge amounts of energy and the outer layers explode – a supernova

An extremely dense neutron star remains

Stars evolve over millions of years and have a finite life span. They form from very large clouds of hydrogen, helium and dust which collapse under gravity. When the temperature in the core of the cloud reaches several million °C the hydrogen is converted to helium in the process of **nuclear fusion**: thermal energy is released when hydrogen nuclei are joined together to form helium nuclei. At the surface of the star the temperature is much lower (around 6000°C for our Sun); energy from the thermonuclear reactions is emitted as **electromagnetic radiation**.

Ⓗ *The evolution of the Universe*

The **big bang theory** is a possible theory for the evolution of the Universe into its present state: an explosion 15 thousand million years ago could have created the matter of the Universe which eventually formed stars grouped in galaxies; the theory explains why we observe galaxies to be moving away from each other.

There is some evidence to support the big bang theory: the wavelength of light from galaxies is 'shifted' towards the red end of the spectrum; the further away the galaxy is, the greater is this **red shift**; this shows that galaxies further away are moving apart more quickly. The age of the Universe can be estimated from the observed rate of expansion.

2 The Earth in the solar system

- ▶ A **year** (approximately 365 days) is the time taken for the Earth to orbit the Sun once.
- ▶ A **day** (24 hours) is the time taken for the Earth to spin once on its own axis.
- ▶ Day and night result from the Earth's rotation on its own axis.
- ▶ The tilt of the Earth's axis relative to the plane of its orbit is the reason for the *seasons* and for the change in the *length of daylight* through the year.
- ▶ The Moon orbits the Earth in just over 27 days; it rotates on its own axis in the same time so the same side always faces us.
- ▶ The *phases of the Moon* repeat every 28 days – a **lunar month** – because of the motion of the Earth–Moon system around the Sun.

Figure 8.2a
How the Earth orbits the Sun

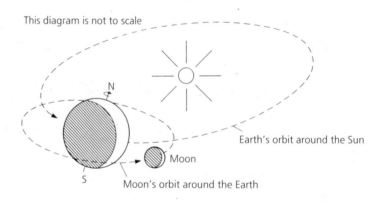

Figure 8.2b
How the seasons are caused

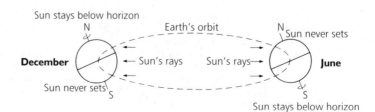

▶ Artificial satellites are used for observation of the Earth, weather monitoring and exploration of the solar system; **geosynchronous** satellites used for communication systems take 24 hours to go round the Equator, so appear stationary.

HINT

Revise your Key Stage 3 notes for more information

3 The Earth's geology

Structure of the Earth – learn where these layers are and their nature: **core, mantle, crust, atmosphere**.

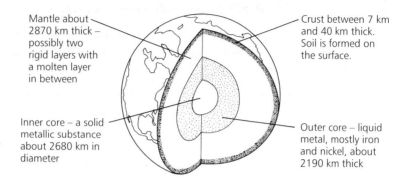

Figure 8.3
Structure of the Earth

Mantle about 2870 km thick – possibly two rigid layers with a molten layer in between

Crust between 7 km and 40 km thick. Soil is formed on the surface.

Inner core – a solid metallic substance about 2680 km in diameter

Outer core – liquid metal, mostly iron and nickel, about 2190 km thick

Types of rock and the rock cycle

There are three types of rock: **igneous, metamorphic** and **sedimentary**.

▶ **Igneous** rocks have interlocking crystals, formed by the cooling and solidifying of hot molten **magma** rising up from the mantle; for example, granite, basalt.

  – Granite (an **intrusive** igneous rock) has large crystals due to slow formation in the Earth's crust.
  – Basalt (an **extrusive** igneous rock) has small crystals due to rapid cooling on the Earth's crust near the surface, often due to volcanic eruption.
▶ **Sedimentary** rocks consist of solid particles bound together by cementing material, formed by deposition of **sediments** which are then buried deeply and compressed; for example, limestone, sandstone. They often contain fossils which provide evidence for the age of the rock.
▶ **Metamorphic** rocks such as slate and marble are formed by the action of extreme *heat and pressure* on existing rocks underground; for example, limestone is changed to marble.

HINT

*Remember – BIG (**b**asalt, **i**gneous, **g**ranite), SS (**s**edimentary **s**andstone), MM (**m**etamorphic **m**arble)*

The **rock cycle** (see Fig. 8.4 below) involves **sedimentary, metamorphic** and **igneous** processes:

▶ **weathering** – physical (water freezing in cracks), chemical (acidic rainwater), biological (roots growing in cracks);
▶ **erosion** (wearing away of rocks by wind and water).

Figure 8.4
The rock cycle

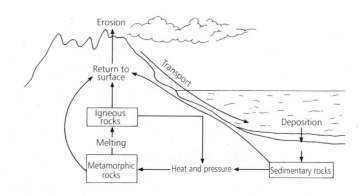

Plate tectonics

The Earth's thin solid crust consists of **plates** which move. **Convection currents** in the mantle, a result of heat released by radioactivity, are a possible cause of plate movement. This movement causes the *formation of mountains, earthquakes* and *volcanic activity* at the plate boundaries. Rocks can be formed and deformed where plates move apart and where volcanoes are active. Rocks can be deformed and sometimes recycled where plates collide or sink below another.

4 The Earth's atmosphere and oceans

The composition of the atmosphere is approximately 80% nitrogen, 20% oxygen, traces of carbon dioxide (0.04%) and the noble gases. The atmosphere has evolved over millions of years:

▶ to begin with the surface of the Earth was molten, then thin crust formed and volcanoes erupted; the atmosphere then contained methane, nitrogen, ammonia, carbon monoxide and steam, but very little oxygen;

▶ primitive plants evolved (on land and in the sea), able to **photosynthesise** and release oxygen: oxygen levels increased;

▶ the **carbon cycle** (see Chapter 4) maintains the composition of the atmosphere: carbon dioxide is *added* by **respiration** and **combustion**, *removed* by **photosynthesis**;

▶ oceans formed as steam condensed.

 The composition of the oceans is maintained by a balance between *input of dissolved salts* in river water (from weathering of rocks) and *removal of dissolved salts*. Removal of salts occurs through:

▶ shell formation by marine organisms

▶ chemical reactions to form sea-floor sediment

▶ crystallisation to form salt deposits

PRACTICE QUESTIONS

Question 1

(a) The following table gives information about some of the planets.

Planet	Distance from the Sun (million kilometres)	Radius (kilometres)	Average density (g cm^{-3})
Earth	149	6350	5.52
Jupiter	773	70960	1.33
Mars	227	3360	3.94
Mercury	58	2400	5.43
Uranus	2886	25275	1.30
Venus	108	6025	5.24
Neptune	4469	25200	1.76

Use the information given in the table to answer the following questions.

(i) On which of these planets is the surface temperature likely to be the lowest?

....(1)

(ii) Which of the planets is closest to the Earth?

....(1)

(iii) What pattern is there between the size and density of the planets?

....

....(1)

(iv) What pattern is there between the density of the planets and their position in the Solar System?

....

....(1)

(b) (i) Explain how stars form from large gas clouds.

....

....

....

....(3)

(ii) Use words from the following list to show the Sun's likely evolution.

   neutron star   red giant   supernova   white dwarf

   Sun $\longrightarrow$ .... $\longrightarrow$ ....   (2)

(iii) Name and explain the process by which energy is produced in the core of the Sun.

....

....

....

....(3)

(c) The colour of light depends upon its wavelength.

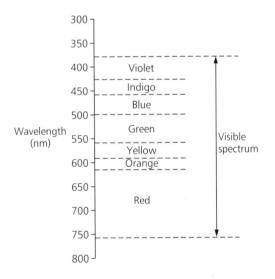

The centre of a star is very hot. It emits light of all wavelengths (colours). As light from the centre of the star passes through the outer layers some wavelengths of light are absorbed.

Different elements absorb light of different wavelengths. By examining the light from a star, astronomers are able to say which elements are present in the star.

The following diagram shows part of the pattern of light which astronomers see if sodium is present in the outer layers of the star.

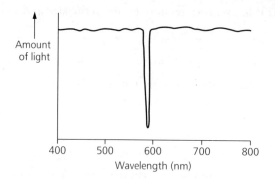

(i) At what wavelength does sodium absorb light?

....nm   (1)

(ii) What colour is this light?

....(1)

(d) Elements absorb several different wavelengths of light. This provides a
    'fingerprint' which can be used to identify the element. The following
    diagrams show the fingerprint of an element measured on Earth and in the
    light from a star in a distant galaxy.

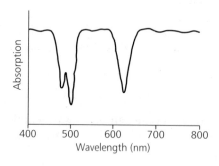   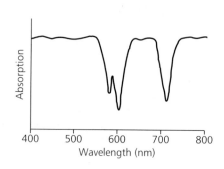

(i) What has happened to the fingerprint of light from the distant star?

    ....

    ....

    ....(1)

(ii) Explain how this, and similar observations, support the Big Bang
     theory of the origin of the Universe.

    ....

    ....

    ....

    ....

    ....

    ....

    ....

    ....

    ....(4)

                                                            (Total marks 19)
                                                                   London

Question 2

(a) Convection currents occur in the molten mantle of the Earth.
    The diagram represents the structure of the inside of the Earth.

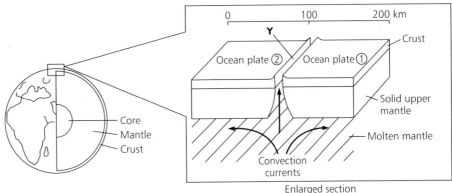

Enlarged section

(i) Describe what you might expect to find at **Y**.

....

....(1)

(ii) Suggest *two* effects that the convection currents would have on the
     ocean plates.

....

....

....

....(2)

(b) The diagrams show how the map of the Earth has changed over the past 200
    million years.

200 million years ago   Today

Suggest how this change could have happened, and what might happen to
the continents during the next 200 million years.

....

....

....

....

....

....(4)

(Total marks 7)
MEG

Question 3

Until fairly recently scientists thought that the continents had always been in the same positions.

Diagram 1 shows where scientists now think the continents were 200 million years ago. Diagram 2 shows the present positions of the continents.

Diagram 1   Diagram 2

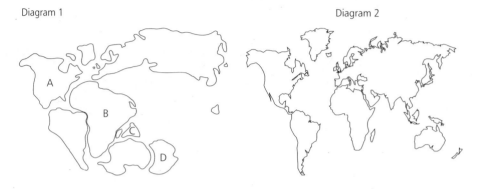

(a) Four land masses have been labelled A, B, C and D on Diagram 1.

Use the same letters, A, B, C and D, *to label on Diagram 2* the present day positions of the four land masses.   (2)

(b) The theory of crustal movement states that the continents have moved apart over the last 200 million years. Give *two* pieces of evidence for this movement.

1. ....

....

2. ....

....(2)

(c) The crust of the Earth includes several tectonic plates.

What causes tectonic plates to move?

....

....

....

....(3)

(d) The tectonic plate labelled D in Diagram 1 eventually collided with an oceanic tectonic plate.

Describe what happens to tectonic plates when they collide.

....

....

....

....

....(4)

(Total marks 11)
NEAB

Electricity and magnetism

TOPIC OUTLINE AND REVISION TIPS

1 Energy and potential difference in electrical circuits

▶ **Electric current** is the flow of charged particles around a circuit of conducting material; in solid metal conductors, current is a flow of *negatively charged electrons*; in an electrolyte (Chapter 6) it is a flow of *positive* and *negative ions*.

▶ The **energy** given to electrons to push them around an electrical circuit is transferred from an electrical source, such as battery, solar cells or a generator, to **components** in the circuit, such as lamps, resistors, bells, motors, LEDs and buzzers; the energy transferred makes things happen in the circuit, e.g. light, heat, sound.

▶ Current is measured in **amperes** (amps: A) by an **ammeter** in the circuit; the current will depend on the **voltage** of the electrical source (e.g. on the number of cells) and on the number and type of components.

The diagrams show the possible positions of an ammeter to measure current in a **series** and in a **parallel** circuit.

Figure 9.1
Current in series and parallel circuits

▶ The current is the same in all parts of a series circuit; in a parallel circuit the current flowing into a junction is the same as the current flowing from the junction.

▶ Some electrical symbols you should know:

Figure 9.2
Some of the conventional symbols for circuit diagrams

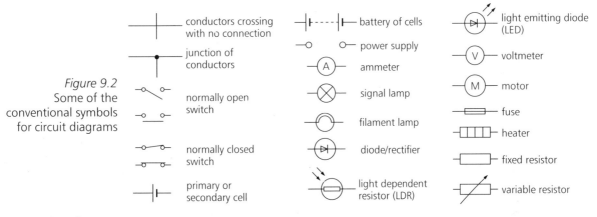

Figure 9.3
The voltmeter is in parallel with the lamp

Measuring the voltage across a component

The **potential difference** (p.d.) or **voltage** across a component in a circuit is a measure of the electrical energy transferred to the component. It is measured in **volts** (V) by a **voltmeter** connected in parallel with the component. For example, when current flows through a lamp, a voltmeter measures the change of electrical energy to light and heat. The voltage is the same across all components connected in parallel.

Potential difference (or voltage) is the number of **joules** of energy transferred for each **coulomb** of charge passed (the *volt* is a *joule per coulomb*): for example, a 6 V power supply transfers 6 joules of energy to each coulomb of charge.

$$\text{energy transferred} = \text{potential difference} \times \text{charge}$$
$$\text{(joule, J)} \qquad\qquad \text{(volt, V)} \qquad\qquad \text{(coulomb, C)}$$

Using this equation, how many joules of electrical energy are changed into light and heat when a charge of 5 C is passed through a lamp which has a p.d. of 12 V across it? $12 \times 5 = 60$ J

Calculating electric charge

The relationship between electric charge, current and time is shown by:

$$\text{charge} = \text{current} \times \text{time} \qquad\qquad Q = I \times t$$
$$\text{(coulomb, C)} \quad \text{(ampere, A)} \quad \text{(second, s)}$$

Using this equation, how many joules of electrical energy are changed to light and heat when a current of 2 A flows for 10 s through a lamp which has a p.d. of 12 V?

Firstly, calculate the charge in coulombs: $2 \times 10 = 20$ C.
Then calculate the energy in joules: $20 \times 12 = 240$ J.

Resistance

▶ The size of the current in a circuit depends on the voltage of the supply and on the **resistance** of the components: the current will change as a result of a change in resistance.

▶ **Resistance** (measured in **ohms**: Ω) is opposition to the flow of an electric current: the greater the resistance in a circuit, the more energy is needed to push charged particles around the circuit. For example, in the filament of a light bulb, the long, thin wire resists the flow of electrons so electrical energy is dissipated as heat and light; other uses of the heating effect in resistors include hair dryers and immersion heaters.

▶ The resistance of a wire depends on four factors:
 1 *diameter* – thin wires have greater resistance than thick wires;
 2 *length* – long wires have greater resistance than short wires;
 3 *material* – iron has greater resistance than copper;
 4 *temperature* – hotter wires have greater resistance than cooler wires.

▶ **Ohm's Law** states that the current passing through a wire (or resistor) at constant temperature is proportional to the potential difference (voltage) between its ends (across the resistor). So, for a given potential difference, a high resistance wire passes a small current and a low resistance wire passes a large current.

Figure 9.4a
You may have used a circuit like this to investigate Ohm's Law

Figure 9.4b
This graph shows the relationship between current and voltage using a resistor in the circuit

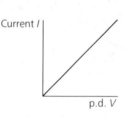

Learn the formula:

$$\text{resistance (ohm, } \Omega) = \frac{\text{potential difference (volt, V)}}{\text{current (ampere, A)}}$$

This can also be written as:

$$\text{voltage} = \text{current} \times \text{resistance} \qquad V = I \times R$$
$$\text{(volt, V)} \qquad \text{(ampere, A)} \qquad \text{(ohm, } \Omega)$$

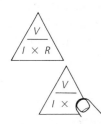

Figure 9.5
A useful way of
learning the formula

Using the formula,

(i) calculate the resistance of a lamp when a p.d. of 12 V across it causes a current of 3 A:

$$R = \frac{V}{I} = \frac{12}{3} = 4\,\Omega$$

(ii) calculate the p.d. across a 10 Ω resistor carrying a current of 3 A:

$$V = I \times R = 3 \times 10 = 30\,V$$

Current–voltage graphs

Current–voltage graphs show how the current varies with voltage in different components.

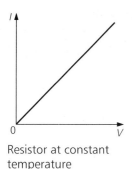

Resistor at constant
temperature

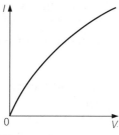

Filament lamp

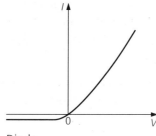

Diode

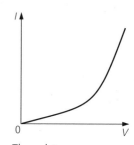

Thermistor

Figure 9.6
Current–voltage graphs

▶ The resistance of a filament lamp increases as the temperature of the filament increases.
▶ A **diode** allows current to pass in one direction but current flow is almost zero in the opposite direction due to a very high resistance.
 ▶ The resistance of a **thermistor** decreases as the temperature increases.
▶ The resistance of a **light-dependent resistor** (**LDR**) decreases as the light intensity increases.

2 Mains electricity

▶ The mains supply is **alternating current** (**a.c.**): the direction of flow changes 50 times per second – its **frequency** is 50 Hz; the voltage is about 230 V a.c.
▶ Batteries supply **direct current** (**d.c.**): the flow is one way.

Figure 9.7a
The trace produced on
a CRO screen by a d.c.
voltage

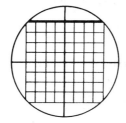

Figure 9.7b
The trace produced on
a CRO screen by an a.c.
voltage

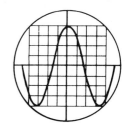

Wiring a plug

Refer to Figure 9.8. Note the following connections:

▶ **live** wire (*brown*) to live (L) pin
▶ **neutral** wire (*blue*) to neutral (N) pin
▶ **earth** wire (*green and yellow*) to earth (E) pin

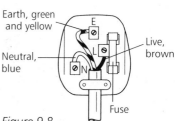

Earth, green
and yellow

Live,
brown

Neutral,
blue

Fuse

Figure 9.8

The earth wire ensures current flows to earth if the appliance becomes faulty, for example if the live wire touches part of the metal casing of the appliance – without the earth wire the current would flow through the person who touched the metal casing.

Calculating the power of an appliance

The **power** of an appliance is the *rate of transfer of electrical energy* to it. It is measured in **watts** (W). 1 watt is the transfer of 1 joule of energy in 1 second. 1 kilowatt (kW) = 1000 watts (W).

Learn the formula:

$$\underset{\text{(watt, W)}}{\text{power}} = \underset{\text{(volt, V)}}{\text{voltage}} \times \underset{\text{(ampere, A)}}{\text{current}}$$

For example, if a lamp on a 230 V household supply has a current of 0.26 A passing through it, its power is $230 \times 0.26 = 60$ W; this means that the lamp is transferring (changing) 60 J of electrical energy into heat and light every second.

Calculating the current used by an appliance

The above formula can be rearranged:

$$\text{current (ampere, A)} = \frac{\text{power (watt, W)}}{\text{voltage (volt, V)}}$$

For example, what is the current used by a 100 W household lamp on a 230 V supply?

$$\text{current} = \frac{100}{230} = 0.43 \text{ A}$$

Safety measures

▶ **Fuses** are thin pieces of wire which melt and break the circuit if too much current flows in the live wire.

▶ A lamp using less than 1 amp requires a **3 amp** fuse in the plug; an electric kettle using, say, 8 amps requires a **13 amp** fuse.

▶ **Double insulation** is plastic casing which insulates the user from the electric current if the appliance is faulty; an earth wire is not needed.

▶ **Magnetic (residual) circuit breakers** can be used instead of fuses in household circuits: they can be reset once the source of the fault is located.

Paying for electricity

The **kilowatt-hour** (kWh) is the unit used to calculate the cost of buying electricity; 1 kWh is the electrical energy used by a 1 kW appliance in 1 hour.

$$\text{no. of kWh} = \text{power (kW)} \times \text{time (h)}$$

$$\underset{\text{(p)}}{\text{cost of electricity supplied}} = \underset{\text{(kWh)}}{\text{energy transferred}} \times \underset{\text{(p/kWh)}}{\text{price per unit}}$$

For example, if a 2 kW electric fire is used for 3 hours it has used 6 kWh of electrical energy; if 1 kWh costs 10p, the total cost is $6 \times 10 = 60$p.

3 Electric charge

▶ Positive or negative electrostatic charges are produced on materials by *loss or gain of electrons*.

▶ There are *forces of attraction* between *unlike charges* and *forces of repulsion* between *like charges*.

▶ Electrostatic charges ('static') can be generated in everyday situations, for example, by synthetic fabrics rubbing together. If charge builds up on an object and causes a voltage (p.d.) between the object and the Earth, a spark may jump across the gap from the object to any earthed conductor; this can be dangerous, for example sparks from car doors to petrol pumps when filling up with petrol.

4 Electromagnetic forces

▶ Magnets have a **north** (N) pole and a **south** (S) pole:
   – *unlike* magnetic poles *attract* (N–S)
   – *like* magnetic poles *repel* (N–N)(S–S)
▶ A magnet has a **magnetic field** around it; the diagram shows the field around a bar magnet.

Figure 9.9

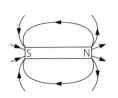

The magnetic field pattern around a magnet

Attraction between unlike poles of two magnets

Repulsion between like poles of two magnets

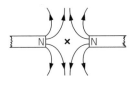

▶ A magnetic field is produced by a current. The diagrams show the magnetic effect of a current in a straight wire and in a **solenoid** (a coil). The current-carrying solenoid has a magnetic field similar to that of a bar magnet: its ends behave as N and S poles.

Figure 9.10
The pattern produced for a single wire carrying current

The current is flowing *upwards* out of the page

The current is flowing *downwards* into the page

The current flows in a *clockwise* direction around the X end of the core

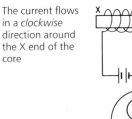

Figure 9.11
The polarity of a solenoid depends on the direction of the current

South pole for a clockwise current

The current flows in an *anticlockwise* direction around the X end of the core

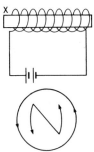

North pole for an anticlockwise current

▶ An **electromagnet** is produced when a soft iron bar is placed inside a solenoid (coil) which has an electric current flowing through it. The strength of an electromagnet can be increased by: increasing the *number of turns* in the coil, and/or increasing the *size of the current* flowing through the coil.
▶ The **d.c. electric motor** is a result of the interaction between the magnetic force around a current-carrying coil and an external magnetic field.

Figure 9.12
The construction of a
simple electric motor

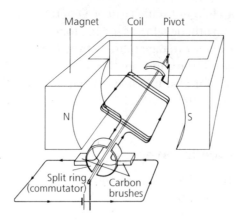

HINT
Look up and learn Fleming's
left-hand rule to predict the
direction of movement of a
current-carrying wire in a
magnetic field

5 Electromagnetic induction

▶ A voltage is induced between the ends of a conductor when there is *relative* movement between the conductor (e.g. a coil) and a magnetic field, or when the magnetic field changes.
▶ The size of the induced voltage is affected by three factors:
  1 *speed*: how fast the magnet or coil is moved;
  2 the *number of turns* in the coil;
  3 the *strength of the magnetic field*.
▶ Electricity can be generated by rotating a magnet inside a coil of wire or by rotating a coil of wire in a magnetic field. This is the principle of an **a.c. generator (alternator)**: the rotation of a coil between magnets induces an alternating voltage which causes an alternating current (a.c.) to flow.

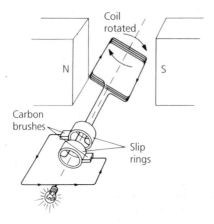

Figure 9.13
The construction of a
simple a.c. generator or
alternator

▶ In a **d.c. generator (dynamo)** the relative rotation of a coil of wire (connected to a split-ring commutator as in a d.c. motor) and a magnetic field produces direct (one way) current (d.c.); a simple version is used to light bicycle lamps.
▶ **Transformers** contain an iron core and two coils of wire, the **primary** and the **secondary**.
▶ When an a.c. voltage is applied across the primary coil of a transformer an a.c. voltage is induced in the secondary coil; the voltage is either **stepped up** (increased) or **stepped down** (decreased).

HINT
Remember, transformers only
work with a.c.

Ⓗ

$$\frac{\text{voltage (primary)}}{\text{voltage (secondary)}} = \frac{\text{turns (primary)}}{\text{turns (secondary)}} \qquad \frac{V_\text{p}}{V_\text{s}} = \frac{n_\text{p}}{n_\text{s}}$$

▶ Electricity is transmitted through power lines in the National Grid at high voltages (400 000 V) so there is a low current and power losses are reduced; step-down transformers reduce the high voltage for domestic use.

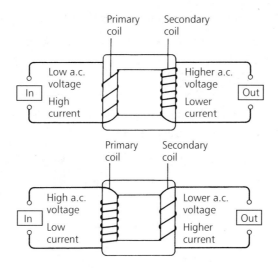

Figure 9.14a
A step-up transformer gives out a higher voltage than the input voltage

Figure 9.14b
A step-down transformer gives out a lower voltage than the input voltage

? PRACTICE QUESTIONS

Question 1

(a) Name *one* electrical appliance in which the main energy transfer is electrical energy to:

   (i) heat energy;

      ....(1)

   (ii) sound energy;

      ....(1)

   (iii) kinetic energy.

      ....(1)

(b) Jean has recently bought an electric lawn mower.

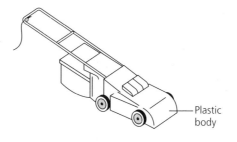

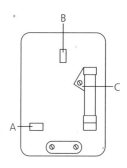

Plastic body

The cable connecting the lawn mower to the mains supply contains only two wires.

   (i) To which parts of the plug should these wires be connected?

      ....

      ....(1)

   (ii) Some electrical appliances have a third wire (green/yellow). State the function of this wire and explain why it is not needed on the lawn mower.

      ....

      ....

      ....

      ....(2)

(c) The lawn mower operates at 240 V and has a power rating of 1250 W.

   (i) Calculate the current required by the lawn mower.

....

....(2)

   (ii) Which of the following fuses should be fitted in the plug? Draw a ring
       around the correct answer.

              1 A   3 A   5 A   13 A   (1)

(d) The following figure shows a transformer.

Core

Primary   Secondary

   (i) What material is used for the transformer coil?

....(1)

   (ii) What happens in the core when the primary coil is switched on?

....(1)

   (iii) What happens in the secondary coil when the primary coil is switched
        on?

....(1)

(Total marks 12)

London

Question 2

The circuit below was used to measure the resistance of a lamp bulb.

(a) The first readings were:

              voltmeter 4.0 V.
              ammeter 1.25 A.

   (i) Calculate the resistance of the lamp at this current.

....

....

                            Resistance = ...Ω   (2)

(ii) If the resistance of the lamp did *not* change, what current would a voltage of 12 V drive through this bulb?

....

....

....

Current = ...A   (2)

(b) Further sets of readings were taken. The resistance of the lamp was calculated for each set of readings.

The graph shows how the resistance of the lamp changes with the current passing through it.

(i)   Explain why the resistance changed with increasing current.

....

....(2)

(ii) Use information from the graph to calculate the potential difference across the lamp when the current is 0.5 A.

....

....

....

....

....

Potential difference = ...V   (3)

(iii) Calculate the power of this lamp when the current passing through it is 0.5 A.

....

....

....

....

....

Power = ...A   (2)

(Total marks 11)

NEAB

Question 3

Diagram 1 shows a perspex rod **before** it is charged.
Diagram 2 shows a perspex rod **after** it is charged.

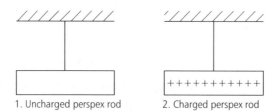

1. Uncharged perspex rod   2. Charged perspex rod

(a) How can you charge a perspex rod?

....

....(1)

(b) Explain how the perspex rod becomes positively charged.

....

....

....(2)

(c) The diagram shows a petrol tanker. It is delivering petrol to a garage.

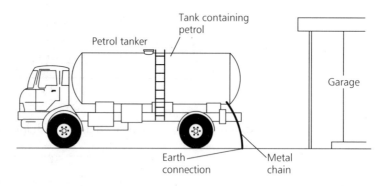

The metal chain prevents a build-up of electrostatic charge on the tanker.
Explain why this is done.

....

....

....

....(2)

(Total marks 5)

London

Question 4

(a) A strip of aluminium is hung between the poles of a magnetic field.

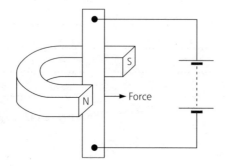

State *two* changes which would increase the size of the force acting on the aluminium strip.

1. ....

2. ....(2)

(b) The drawing shows a coil of wire connected to an ammeter.

When a bar magnet is moved into the coil the needle of the ammeter moves.

(i) Explain why the ammeter gives a reading.

....

....

....(3)

(ii) How could the reading on the meter be increased?

....(1)

(Total marks 6)

NEAB

Question 5

Mark has designed a circuit for measuring the thickness of paper. Diagram 1 shows his circuit, and diagram 2 shows the arrangement of component X and the lamp.

(a) What is component X, shown in the diagrams?

....(1)

(b) Mark placed sheets of paper of different thickness between X and the lamp. His results are shown on the graph overleaf.

Explain why the current changes with the thickness of the paper, as shown by the graph.

....

....

....

....(3)

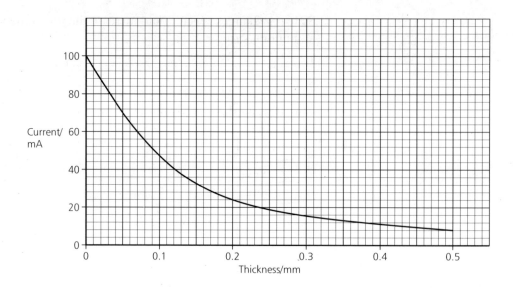

Thickness/mm

(c) When a sheet of unknown thickness is placed between X and the lamp, the ammeter reads 40 mA. Use the information in the graph to find the thickness of this paper.

....(1)

(d) Calculate the resistance of X in ohms when the current is 40 milliamps (mA).

....

....

....

....(4)

(Total marks 9)

London

10 Energy transfer and energy resources

✓ TOPIC OUTLINE AND REVISION TIPS

HINT
Check your notes for examples of energy changes involving different forms of energy. You are often asked about energy transfers involving electrical energy, e.g. an electric kettle transfers electrical energy into heat (thermal energy)

1 Energy transfer

Energy is being transferred from one form to another when you see something happening, e.g. moving: in a clockwork toy potential energy in the wound-up spring is transferred to kinetic energy which turns the wheels.

▶ Energy exists in many forms: **thermal** (heat), **electromagnetic** (e.g. **light, radiant**), **electrical**, **sound**, **kinetic** (movement), **chemical**, **nuclear**, **potential** (**gravitational, elastic**).

▶ During any energy transfer some energy is always changed to non-useful thermal energy: for example, in a battery-operated toy,

$$\text{chemical} \longrightarrow \text{kinetic} \longrightarrow \text{heat and sound}$$

Efficiency of energy transfers

The **efficiency** of an energy transfer is the *useful energy output* as a fraction of the energy input:

$$\text{efficiency} = \frac{\text{useful energy transferred by device (energy output)}}{\text{total energy supplied to device (energy input)}} \times 100\%$$

or $\text{efficiency} = \dfrac{\text{power output}}{\text{power input}} \times 100\%$

For example, a motor is supplied at 100 W and the power output is 60 W;

$$\text{efficiency} = \frac{60 \text{ (power output)}}{100 \text{ (power input)}} \times 100\% = 60\%$$

The other 40% is transferred to the surroundings and is 'wasted'.

The processes of thermal energy transfer

Differences in temperature lead to transfer of energy; thermal energy is transferred in one or more of four processes: **conduction, convection, radiation, evaporation**.

▶ **Conduction:** thermal energy is transferred (conducted) through a solid as a result of particles *vibrating* and (in a metal) free electrons *moving*; energy is transferred from places where the temperature is higher to places where the temperature is lower; limited conduction takes place in liquids and gases.

▶ **Convection:** thermal energy is transferred through a fluid (liquid or gas) by particles *moving* from places where the temperature is higher to places where the temperature is lower, carrying energy; ocean currents and winds are a result of changes in density in liquids and gases which set up **convection currents**.

HINT
Look up in your practical notes details of experiments to show convection currents

▶ **Thermal radiation:** energy is transferred by **infra-red radiation** which can pass through a vacuum and be reflected; radiant energy is emitted from all hot objects which lose heat to their surroundings; the hotter the object the more energy it will radiate; the energy is *absorbed* by cooler objects, raising their temperature. Dark, matt surfaces emit (and absorb) more radiation than light, shiny surfaces.

HINT

In each method of energy transfer be clear about how the particles are behaving

HINT

Make sure you can evaluate the effectiveness and cost effectiveness of methods used to reduce energy consumption

▶ **Evaporation:** the loss of fast-moving particles from the surface of a liquid; the rate of evaporation depends on the *surface area*, the *temperature* of the liquid, the *humidity* and *movement* of surrounding air.

Reducing heat loss

▶ **Insulation** reduces the conduction of energy from hotter to colder objects; many methods of insulation work by trapping air, which is a poor conductor of heat.
▶ Heat losses from buildings can be reduced by various methods of insulation such as double glazing, cavity-wall insulation and loft insulation.

2 Energy resources

▶ The Sun is the original source of most of the Earth's energy transfers.
▶ The effect of the Sun on the atmosphere causes wind and waves.
▶ The Sun's energy is used in photosynthesis by green plants; heat and pressure change the remains of animals and plants into **fossil fuels** over millions of years.

Renewable and non-renewable energy resources

▶ **Non-renewable energy resources** are finite (cannot be replaced): fossil fuels (e.g. coal, oil, gas) and nuclear fuels (e.g. uranium).
▶ **Renewable energy resources** are not finite (can be replaced): biomass (e.g. wood), wind energy, solar energy, hydro-electric energy, tidal energy, wave energy, geothermal energy.
▶ Renewable energy sources will not run out, they involve no fuel costs and produce no pollution.
▶ The table compares advantages and disadvantages of the main renewable sources of energy in the *production of electricity*.

Energy source	Advantages	Disadvantages
Hydro-electric	Reliable in areas of high rainfall High power output Pumped storage allows demand to be matched	Areas of natural beauty may be visually spoilt High cost of construction and maintenance
Wind	High power output possible Useful for isolated communities	Windmills can visually spoil the environment Wind speeds may vary, so the generation of electricity is unpredictable
Solar	Useful for isolated communities	Cloud cover blocks the sun Huge solar panels needed which are expensive to build
Tidal	Reliable High power output possible	Expensive to build barrages May cause silting up of rivers
Geothermal	Long-term supplies can provide hot water	Not widely available Costly to install and maintain
Wave	Useful for isolated island communities	Many technological problems Hazard to shipping

▶ In a conventional **thermal power station** fuel, such as coal or oil, is burnt to heat water and produce steam; the high pressure steam turns huge turbines which spin round and in turn drive a generator which produces alternating current.

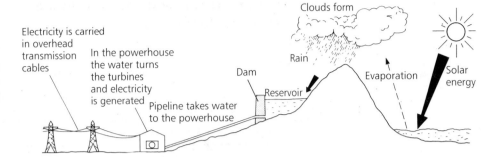

Figure 10.1
How electricity is
generated from hydro-
electric energy

PRACTICE QUESTIONS

Question 1
Electricity can be generated in several different ways.

(a) Describe how the energy in coal is transferred to drive generators in coal-fired power stations.

....

....

....

....

....

....(3)

(b) The diagram shows a section through a tidal power generating system.

Describe fully how this method of driving turbines to generate electricity is *different* from using coal.

....

....

....

....

....

....(2)

(c) Compare in detail the advantages and disadvantages of these two methods of generating electricity.

....

....

....

....

....

....

....

....

....

....

....

....(8)

(Total marks 13)

NEAB

Question 2

(a) Give *one* example of a non-renewable energy source.

....(1)

(b) (i) Give *one* example of a renewable energy source.

....(1)

   (ii) Explain how this energy source is used to produce electricity.

   ....

   ....

   ....(2)

(c) Explain how the Sun is the original source of the energy in a fossil fuel such as coal.

....

....

....(2)

(d) The following diagram shows the different stages in a gas-fired power station.

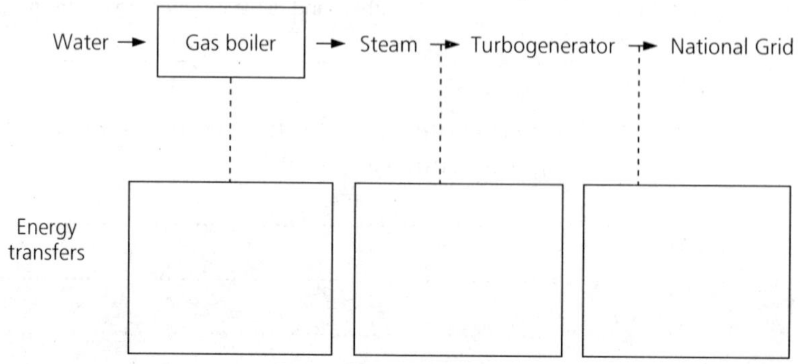

Figure 10.3

Water → | Gas boiler | → Steam → Turbogenerator → National Grid

Energy transfers

In the boxes provided, state the energy transfers which take place.   (3)

(Total marks 9)

London

11 Forces and motion

1 Force and acceleration

HINT
*Remember **s**peed is a **s**calar quantity: **ss***

HINT
Check your notes for any distance–time graphs you have plotted from ticker-tape measurements

HINT
*Remember **v**elocity is a **v**ector quantity: **vv***

▶ **Speed** is the distance travelled in a unit of time. It is a **scalar** quantity: it has a **magnitude** (size) but not direction.

Learn the formula:

$$\text{speed (m/s)} = \frac{\text{distance travelled (m)}}{\text{time taken (s)}} \qquad s = \frac{d}{t}$$

For example, if a car travels 300 km in 6 hours, its average speed = 300/6 = 50 km/h.

▶ **Velocity** is the distance travelled in unit time in a *stated direction*. It is a **vector** quantity: it has magnitude *and* direction; the direction must be stated, e.g. a force of 20 N acting vertically downwards.

▶ The slope of a distance–time graph represents velocity: for example a car travelling with uniform (constant) velocity covers equal distances in equal times; on a distance–time graph this is shown as a straight line.

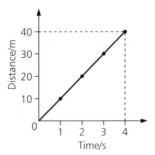

Figure 11.1
A distance–time graph showing uniform velocity

On this graph you can see that a distance of 40 m is travelled in 4 s, so the speed is 40/4 = 10 m/s.

▶ **Acceleration** is the change in velocity per unit time (rate of change of velocity).

Learn the formula:

$$\text{acceleration} = \frac{\text{change in velocity}}{\text{time taken for change}} \qquad a = \frac{(v-u)}{t}$$

For example, a steady increase in velocity from 30 m/s to 60 m/s in 5 seconds gives

Ⓗ
$$\text{acceleration} = \frac{(60 - 30)\,\text{m/s}}{5\,\text{s}} = 6\,\text{m/s per second}$$

▶ Positive acceleration involves an increase in velocity; negative acceleration (deceleration) involves a decrease in velocity.

▶ The slope of a velocity–time graph represents acceleration.

▶ The area under a velocity–time graph measures the distance travelled.

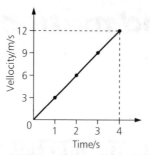

Figure 11.2
A velocity–time graph
showing uniform
acceleration

For this graph the distance travelled is the area of the lower triangle:
area = $\frac{1}{2} \times$ base $\times$ height = $\frac{1}{2} \times 4 \times 12 = 24$ m.

Forces acting on a moving object or an object at rest

▶ An object at rest requires a **force** to make it move and accelerate. A moving
object requires a force to make it speed up, slow down, or to stop it. The size
of the force required depends on the mass of the object.

Learn the formula:

$$\text{force} = \text{mass} \times \text{acceleration} \qquad F = m \times a$$
$$\quad\text{(N)} \quad\quad \text{(kg)} \quad\quad\quad \text{(m/s}^2\text{)}$$

▶ The magnitude of the acceleration produced depends on the *size of the force*
(N) and the *mass of the object* (kg).

$$a = \frac{F}{m}$$

The acceleration doubles if the force doubles or if the mass is halved.
For example:
if a force of 15 N acts on a mass of 3 kg then acceleration = 5 m/s^2,
but if a force of 30 N acts on a mass of 3 kg then acceleration = 10 m/s^2.

Friction

▶ **Friction** is a force that resists motion; it acts in the opposite direction. Friction
allows tyres to grip the road; air resistance allows a parachute to slow down a
falling sky diver.
▶ Friction causes an increase in temperature: kinetic energy is transferred to
thermal energy (heat). It also causes wear of surfaces. Unwanted friction can
be reduced, e.g. by oil in engines, ball bearings between wheel and axle.

Factors affecting a vehicle's stopping distance

The distance over which a moving vehicle will come to rest (thinking
distance + braking distance) is determined by a number of factors:

1 *speed* of the vehicle: e.g. car A and car B of the same mass, car A travelling at
   twice the speed of car B needs *four times* the stopping distance;
2 *mass* of the vehicle: e.g. car A and car B travelling at same speed, car A *twice the
   mass* of car B needs *twice* the stopping distance;
3 *friction* between the tyres and the road: e.g. less friction on a wet/icy road
   lengthens the stopping distance;
4 *friction* between the tyres and the brakes: e.g. smooth tyres or faulty brakes
   reduce the stopping force and lengthen the braking distance;
5 *reaction time* of driver: the 'thinking time' is affected by concentration, alcohol
   intake, tiredness.

Pairs of forces

When two bodies interact, the forces they exert on each other are *equal and
opposite*; this means when object A pulls or pushes object B then object B pulls

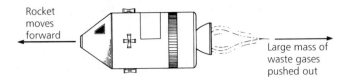

Figure 11.3
The rocket accelerates
due to the force of the
gases being pushed out

or pushes object A with an equal force in the opposite direction. For example, a rocket moves forward due to the force of the waste gases from the engine being pushed behind: the force on the rocket is equal and opposite to the force on the waste gases.

2 Forces acting on falling objects

▶ **Gravity** is the downward force acting on free-falling objects and is caused by the Earth's gravitational field.

▶ The **weight** of an object is the force of gravity which acts on it towards the centre of the Earth.

▶ The greater the **gravitational field strength** and/or the greater the mass of an object, the greater its weight:

$$\text{weight} = \text{mass} \times \text{gravitational field strength}$$
$$\text{(N)} \qquad \text{(kg)} \qquad\qquad \text{(N/kg)}$$

A mass of 1 kg has a weight of approximately 10 N on Earth: the Earth's gravitational field strength is approximately 10 N/kg.

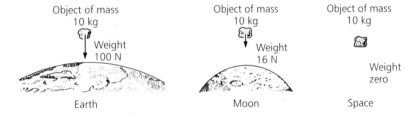

Figure 11.4
The mass of the object
stays the same but the
weight changes

▶ **Terminal velocity** is the constant velocity reached by falling objects in air or fluids.

▶ The terminal velocity is affected by **frictional resistance** (drag) and by the shape of the object (streamlined objects fall faster).

▶ Air resistance opposes the motion of an object falling through the air; the resistance increases as the speed increases and so the acceleration of the object is reduced; eventually air resistance (exerted upwards) equals the weight of the object (acting downwards) so the **resultant** force on the object is zero as the two opposing forces balance; the object then falls at constant velocity (the terminal velocity); for example, a free-fall sky diver has a terminal velocity of about 160 km/h.

3 Work, power and energy

▶ **Work** is done and **energy transferred** when a force moves an object through a distance, and when a force acts to stop an object moving.

$$\text{energy transferred in joules (J)} = \text{work done in joules (J)}$$

▶ *Learn the formula:*

$$\text{work done} = \text{force} \times \text{distance moved} \qquad W = F \times d$$
$$\text{(J)} \qquad \text{(N)} \qquad \text{(m)}$$

For example, a person pushes a box with a force of 300 N a distance of 20 m: the work done = $300 \times 20 = 600$ J.

- **Power** is the rate of doing work or of transferring energy.

$$\text{power (W)} = \frac{\text{work done (energy transferred) (J)}}{\text{time taken (s)}} = \frac{F \times d}{t}$$

For example, a person takes 20 seconds to lift 5 boxes up to a shelf 2 m high using a force of 50 N per box:

$$\text{work done} = 50 \text{ (N)} \times 2 \text{ (m)} \times 5 \text{ (boxes)} = 500 \text{ J}$$

$$\text{power developed} = \frac{500 \text{ (J)}}{20 \text{ (s)}} = 25 \text{ W}$$

- The gravitational force acting on a mass is approximately 10 N/kg, so if you are given the mass (in kg) of an object in a calculation multiply the figure by 10 to obtain the vertical force. For example, a person of mass 60 kg climbs 4 m in 5 seconds:

$$\text{work done} = 60 \text{ (kg)} \times 10 \text{ (N/kg)} \times 4 \text{ (m)} = 2400 \text{ J}$$

$$\text{power developed} = \frac{2400 \text{ (J)}}{5 \text{ (s)}} = 480 \text{ W}$$

- **Gravitational potential energy** is the energy an object has as a result of its position; it depends on the *mass* of the object and its *height* above the ground. The formula is:

(H)

$$\text{gravitational potential energy} = \text{mass} \times g \times \text{height}$$
$$= m \times g \times h$$

where g is the gravitational field strength (approximately 10 N/kg). For example, the potential energy gained by the person climbing 4 m is 60 kg $\times$ 10 N/kg $\times$ 4 m = 2400 J. Note this is equal to the work done against the force of gravity.

- **Kinetic energy** is the energy of motion; it depends on the *mass* of a moving object and the *velocity*.
  The formula is:

(H)

$$\text{kinetic energy} = \tfrac{1}{2} \times \text{mass} \times (\text{velocity})^2 = \tfrac{1}{2} \times m \times v^2$$

The greater the mass and/or velocity, the greater the kinetic energy. If the *velocity doubles* the kinetic energy increases *four times*: for example, the kinetic energy of a person of mass 60 kg travelling with a velocity of 2 m/s = $\tfrac{1}{2} \times 60 \text{ kg} \times (2 \text{ m/s})^2 = 120 \text{ J}$; if the velocity is doubled to 4 m/s the kinetic energy $= \tfrac{1}{2} \times 60 \text{ kg} \times (4 \text{ m/s})^2 = 480 \text{ J}$.

(H) - For a falling object the loss of potential energy is equal to the gain in kinetic energy, assuming work done against frictional resistance is negligible.

4 Force and pressure on solids, liquids and gases

- **Pressure** is the effect of force on an area; the units are **pascals** (Pa) or N/m².

$$\text{pressure (Pa)} = \frac{\text{force (N)}}{\text{area (m}^2\text{)}}$$

- The pressure in a fluid depends on the *depth* in the fluid and the *density* of the fluid. Dam walls are constructed with wide bases to resist the increased pressure at greater depth.

Hydraulic systems
Hydraulic brakes use liquid pressure to transfer a force from one place to another. Three principles are involved in hydraulic systems:

1 liquids *cannot be compressed* (squashed);
2 liquids transmit pressure *equally in all directions*;
3 any change in pressure is transmitted to *all parts* of the liquid.

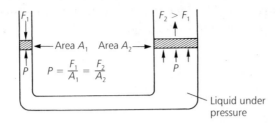

Figure 11.5
Principle of hydraulic systems

Liquid under pressure

▶ A small force applied to the piston of a brake pedal cylinder is *multiplied* to become a large force applied to the pistons of the brake cylinders.
▶ Hydraulic systems would fail if gases entered the hydraulic fluid; gases can be compressed and so pressure would not be transmitted through the fluid.

> **HINT**
>
> *Also revise from your notes details of Hooke's Law experiments about how extension varies with applied force for helical springs, rubber bands and copper wires*

Pressure of a gas

▶ The particles in a gas move very fast and exert forces (and therefore pressure) on the walls of a container.
▶ The pressure of a gas can be increased by:
  – *increasing the temperature* so the particles have more kinetic energy and move faster, exerting a greater force on the walls of the container;
  – *reducing the volume* of the gas – the particles have less space to move in so collide with the walls of the container more often.

PRACTICE QUESTIONS

Question 1

(a) Peter cycles from home to school. The following graph represents the journey.

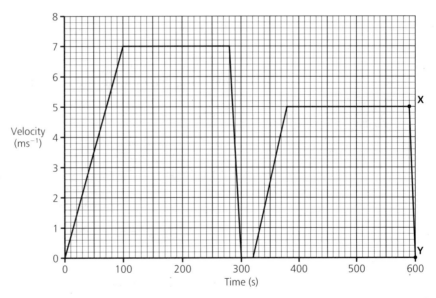

(i) What is Peter's velocity after 50 s?

....(1)

(ii) After how many seconds does Peter stop at some traffic lights?

....(1)

(iii) Calculate Peter's deceleration, in m/s², between points **X** and **Y**.

....

....

Deceleration = ...m/s² (2)

(iv) Peter and his bicycle have a combined mass of 60 kg. Calculate the resultant force exerted on Peter and his bicycle as he decelerates between points **X** and **Y**.

....

....

....(2)

(b) (i) After his journey, Peter noticed that his bicycle tyres, and the air they contained, were warm. Explain why.

....

....(1)

(ii) Explain what effect, if any, this has on the force exerted on the walls of the tyres.

....

....

....

....(2)

(c) Peter's bicycle has both a dynamo and a battery to power his bicycle lamps. The dynamo produces electricity when turned by the wheel.

(i) Suggest *one* advantage and *one* disadvantage of using a dynamo rather than a battery to power the bicycle lamps.

Advantage ....

....

Disadvantage ....

....(2)

(ii) The following diagram shows the structure of the dynamo.

Describe how the dynamo works.

....

....

....

....(2)

(d) The dynamo and battery are connected together in the following circuit. When Peter is travelling at normal speed, the dynamo produces a greater voltage than the battery.

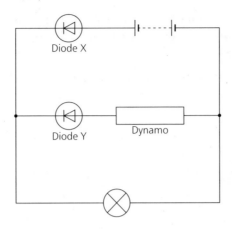

Suggest how this circuit works.

....

....

....

....(4)

(Total marks 17)

London

Question 2

The diagram below shows a braking system on a modern car. The cylinder and pipes are filled with a liquid called brake fluid. When the driver pushes the brake pedal it pushes the liquid down the brake pipes and makes the brakes work. This type of system relies on the fact that liquids cannot be compressed (squeezed up).

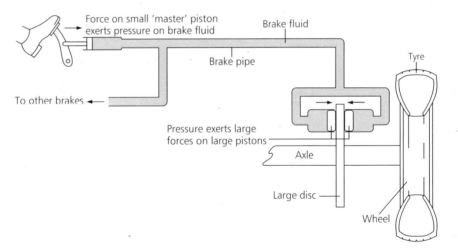

(a) The diagram below labelled **A** shows how molecules are arranged in a gas such as air.

Complete diagram **B** by showing how molecules would be arranged in a liquid such as brake fluid.

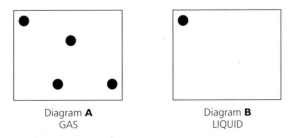

(2)

(b) Car brakes become very dangerous if air gets into the system because they do not work properly. (You have to press the brake pedal a long way to make the brakes work.)

Explain why the brakes do not work properly when a lot of air gets into the pipes.

....

....

....

....(2)

(Total marks 4)

NEAB

Question 3

The overall stopping distance for a moving car is the sum of the thinking distance and the braking distance.

Braking distance   Thinking
                          distance

(a) Explain how a worn tyre can have a *big* effect on the stopping distance.

....

....

....

....(3)

(b) A car of mass 1000 kg travels at a steady velocity (v).

(i) It has a kinetic energy of 242 kJ. What is the velocity of the car?

Kinetic energy $= \frac{1}{2}mv^2$

....

....

....

....(3)

(ii) The car is brought to rest in a braking distance of 40 m. Calculate the average braking force.

....

....

....(3)

(Total marks 9)

London

12 Waves

✓ **TOPIC OUTLINE AND REVISION TIPS**

1 Characteristics of waves

▶ Waves transfer energy without transferring matter.

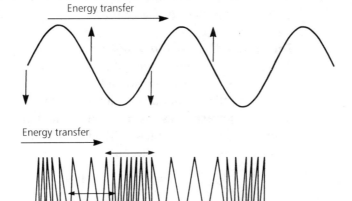

Figure 12.1a
Energy is being transferred along this transverse wave, but the particles only move up and down

Figure 12.1b
Energy is being transferred along this longitudinal wave, but the particles are oscillating from left to right

▶ There are two types of wave: **longitudinal** (e.g. sound waves which need a medium to travel through) and **transverse** (e.g. electromagnetic waves which can travel through a vacuum).

Reflection, refraction and diffraction

All waves can be **reflected**, **refracted** and **diffracted**.

▶ **Reflection** is a change of direction (bouncing back) when a wave strikes a boundary; if a wave hits a plane surface at an angle it is *reflected at the same angle* away from the surface.

angle of incidence (i) = angle of reflection (r)

Light is reflected from a mirror in this way; an image is seen behind the mirror.

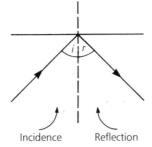

Figure 12.2a
The angle of incidence equals the angle of reflection

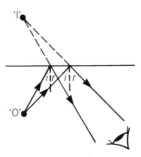

Figure 12.2b
The image 'I' of the object 'O' appears behind the mirror

▶ **Refraction** is a change of direction (bending) when a wave passes from one medium to another; for example when light passes from air to glass the direction changes due to a decrease in speed (see Fig. 12.3 overleaf).

▶ **Diffraction** is a spreading out of waves when they pass through a narrow gap or past an obstacle. The shape of the **wavefront** changes so that it spreads out around the edges of the gap or obstacle. Velocity, wavelength and frequency are unchanged. Everyday applications include water waves passing through

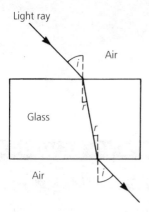

Figure 12.3
The light ray is bent or
'refracted' as it enters
and leaves the glass

the opening of a harbour, radio waves passing around mountains, sound waves passing through doorways.

Total internal reflection of light

This occurs when incident light rays are completely reflected inside a medium such as glass: for example, when light passes through a glass fibre it is totally internally reflected (bounced) along the fibre; this principle is used in **optical fibre communication systems** to carry telephone messages and other digital information as pulses of light. Totally reflecting **prisms** are used in binoculars, periscopes and vehicle reflectors.

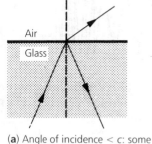 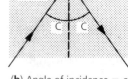 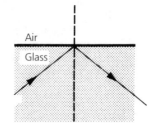

Figure 12.4a–c
Light is totally reflected
inside a medium when
the incident angle is
greater than the critical
angle c

(**a**) Angle of incidence < c: some refraction, some reflection

(**b**) Angle of incidence = c: refraction at 90°

(**c**) Angle of incidence > c: total internal reflection

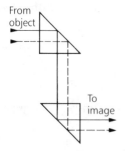

Figure 12.5
Periscope

The spectrum

White light passing through a prism is **dispersed** to give a range of colours: the **spectrum**. Light waves of different wavelengths (colours) are refracted (bent) by different amounts (red least, violet most) because they travel through the prism at different speeds.

Figure 12.6
White light is split into
a spectrum of colours
as it passes through the
prism

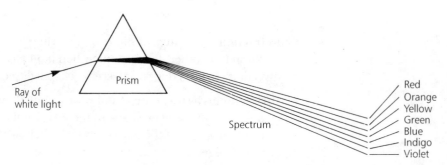

It is the retina of the eye that is sensitive to different wavelengths of light, allowing us to distinguish colours. The structure of the eye is dealt with in Chapter 1 (p. 9).

Frequency, wavelength and amplitude of a wave

All waves have the following characteristics:

▶ **frequency** – the number of complete cycles per second, unit the **hertz** (Hz);
▶ **wavelength** – e.g. the distance between two peaks;
▶ **amplitude** – the size of the wave, e.g. the maximum distance a particle is displaced.

Figure 12.7
The letter '*a*' shows the amplitude of the wave. The letter '*λ*' shows the wavelength

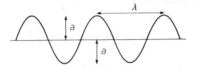

Figure 12.8

A low frequency wave   A high frequency wave

▶ A useful formula to learn:

$$\text{speed} = \text{frequency} \times \text{wavelength} \qquad v = f \times \lambda$$
$$\text{(m/s)} \qquad \text{(Hz)} \qquad \text{(m)}$$

For example, a wave with a frequency of 30 Hz and a wavelength of 3 m is travelling at a speed of 90 m/s.

2 The electromagnetic spectrum

Electromagnetic radiation consists of transverse waves with a range of frequencies and wavelengths. These waves can travel through a vacuum (no material medium is required). They all travel at the same speed in air or a vacuum: 300 000 000 metres per second.

The chart below summarises the waves of the electromagnetic spectrum.

Type of wave	Uses	Source	Wavelength Frequency
Radio waves	Radio broadcasting and communication, television	Alternating current in radio transmitters	long low
Microwaves	Cooking in microwave ovens, radar, satellite communications	Oscillating electronic circuits	
Infra-red waves	Electric fires, remote-control devices, thermal imaging	Any hot object	
Visible light	Electric lights, photography, optical fibre communications	Very hot objects, lasers	
Ultra-violet waves	Sunbeds, fluorescent lamps, illuminating security markings	Glowing gases	
X-rays	Medical photography, security at airports	X-ray tubes	
Gamma rays	Killing cancer cells, sterilisation of equipment and food	Radioactive materials	short high

Effects of electromagnetic radiation on the human body

▶ Microwaves are absorbed by the water in cells, causing internal heating of body tissue; the heat may damage or kill cells.

▶ Infra-red waves are absorbed by the skin and felt as heat; excess may burn the skin.

▶ Ultra-violet radiation passes through the upper layer of the skin in the absence of pigment and may damage cells leading to sunburn and possible skin cancer (melanoma); exposure of the eyes can cause blindness.

▶ X-radiation and gamma radiation penetrates living tissue and may cause cells to become cancerous or to be destroyed.

3 Sound and ultrasound

Sound waves

▶ Sound waves are longitudinal pressure waves produced by a vibrating source.

▶ They require a medium (e.g. air) to travel through (cannot travel through a vacuum).

▶ They travel faster the denser the medium.

▶ They can be reflected, refracted and diffracted.

▶ **Echoes** are produced when sound waves are reflected from a hard surface.

▶ The **amplitude** of the wave is a measure of the **loudness** of a sound.

> **HINT**
>
> *Loudness–amplitude – remember la!*

Figure 12.9
A loud sound has a large amplitude. A high pitch sound has a high frequency and a short wavelength

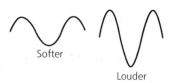
Softer
Louder

Low pitch

High pitch

▶ The **frequency** is a measure of the **pitch** of a sound.

▶ Sounds detected by the human ear have frequencies in the range 20–20 000 Hz.

▶ Microphones change sound waves into electric current.

▶ Loudspeakers change electric current to sound waves.

> **HINT**
>
> *Look in your notes for information about harmful effects of noise pollution and how these effects can be reduced (e.g. ear defenders, double glazing, acoustic tiles)*

The ear

The ear detects the pressure variations of a sound wave.

Learn the name and function of:

▶ **ear drum** – responds to the pressure wave by vibrating

▶ **ossicles** – three small bones to which vibrations are passed

▶ **cochlea** – coiled tube in the inner ear filled with fluid to which vibrations are passed, and containing nerve endings

▶ **auditory nerve** – carries impulses to the brain

Figure 12.10
The structure of the ear

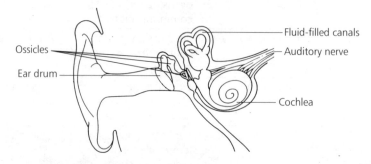

Ossicles

Ear drum

Fluid-filled canals

Auditory nerve

Cochlea

Ultrasonic waves

These are produced by electronic oscillators. They are sound waves of very high frequency (> 20 000 Hz: above the audible range for humans).
Ultrasonic waves are used by:

▶ hospitals for *antenatal screening* (scanning) of a foetus to check development;

▶ ships and submarines for *determining depth* of water;
▶ bats for *direction finding*.

Ⓗ 4 Seismic waves

Seismic waves are vibrations in the Earth (shock waves) due to an earthquake; they may be longitudinal or transverse.

▶ Longitudinal (P) waves travel quickly through liquids and solids.
▶ Transverse (S) waves travel more slowly, only through solids.
▶ Both P and S waves travel more quickly the denser the material.

Analysis of the wave records produced by seismic waves provides evidence for the different layers of the Earth (see Fig. 8.3, p. 63).

PRACTICE QUESTIONS

Question 1
The diagram below shows a human ear, with a sound wave approaching it.

(a) Show, by a line, the path taken by the sound energy as it enters the ear from the point X until it reaches the auditory nerve Y.   (1)

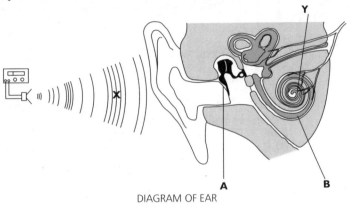

DIAGRAM OF EAR

(b) Name the parts labelled A and B in the diagram.

A   ....

B   ....   (2)

(c) The diagrams A, B, C and D below all represent sound waves drawn to the same scale.

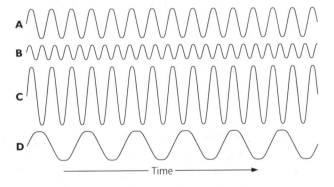

Which diagram, A, B, C or D, represents:

(i) the loudest sound? ....

(ii) the sound with the highest pitch? ....   (2)

(Total marks 5)

NEAB

Question 2

(a) The diagram below shows a ray of sunlight falling on the side of a prism at the point P. A screen is drawn on the other side of the prism. On leaving the prism the sunlight forms a visible spectrum on the screen between the points X and Y.

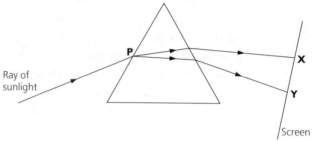

(i) Name *one* type of radiation to be found:

　　1. above X. ....

　　2. below Y. ....(2)

(ii) Give *one* use of:
　　UV radiation;...

　　..

　　microwaves. ....

　　...(2)

(b) (i) Name a part of the electromagnetic spectrum which is used to sterilize surgical instruments.

　　..(1)

(ii) Explain how this radiation sterilizes surgical instruments.

　　..

　　...(1)

(Total marks 6)
NEAB

Question 3

(a)

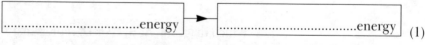

The pupil is using a microphone connected to an oscilloscope.

An oscilloscope can be used to display a sound wave as a wave on its screen.

(i) What is the useful energy transfer which takes place when a microphone is used?

　　.....................................energy ➤ ....energy　(1)

(ii) What is the useful energy transfer which takes place when an oscilloscope is used?

　　.....................................energy ➤ ....energy　(1)

(iii) A microphone is an example of a transducer. What does a transducer do?

A transducer is a device which ....

....

....(1)

(b) The following diagram shows a regular wave.

Which letter, **A**, **B**, **C**, **D**, **E** or **F** shows:

(i)   the amplitude;   ....

(ii) a crest or peak;   ....

(iii) a trough;   ....

(iv) the wavelength?   ....   (4)

(c) Complete the following sentence.

The frequency of a regular wave means the ....

....(1)

(d) The amplitude, the frequency and the wavelength of a sound wave can all be changed.

(i)   What change, or changes, would you have to make so that the sound would be quieter?

....(1)

(ii) What change, or changes, would you have to make so that the sound would be lower in pitch?

....(1)

(e) Explain how a stringed instrument, such as a guitar or a violin, produces sound waves.

....

....

....

....(4)

(Total marks 14)

SEG

Question 4

(a) National television and radio broadcasts are transmitted from the Telecom tower, a very tall building in London. The sound and picture information is carried by microwaves which cannot be detected by a domestic radio or television set. One reason for using microwaves is that they are more easily focused into a narrow beam.

Describe *one* similarity and *one* difference between microwaves and the radio waves which are detected by a domestic radio.

....

....(2)

(b) Repeater stations receive the microwaves and send them on to other repeater stations. Repeater stations are necessary because the microwaves cannot be received more than 50 km from their source. The figure below shows part of the network of repeater stations around the south of England.

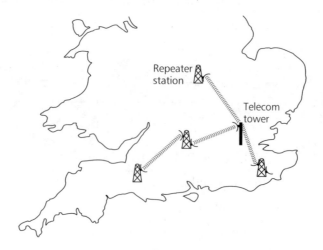

(i) Explain why the microwaves cannot travel long distances over the Earth's surface.

....

....(2)

(ii) Suggest why the microwaves are transmitted as a narrow beam.

....

....(2)

(c) Microwaves used in cooking have a wavelength of 12 cm and travel at a speed of 300 000 000 m/s.

(i) Use a labelled diagram to explain the meaning of the phrase 'a wavelength of 12 cm'.

(2)

(ii) Calculate the *frequency* of the microwaves used in cooking.

....

....

....

....

....(4)

(Total marks 12)

MEG

Radioactivity

13

1 Radioactivity

▶ Radioactivity arises from the *breakdown of unstable nuclei* in some atoms.
▶ The process is known as **radioactive decay**.
▶ Energy is released as **gamma rays** or as kinetic energy of **alpha** and **beta particles**, collectively called **nuclear radiation**.
▶ Some **isotopes** (e.g. carbon-14, uranium-235) are unstable and decay by radioactive emissions to a more stable form, which may be a new element.
▶ Radioactivity can be detected by photographic film or a **Geiger-Müller (GM) tube**.

2 Background radiation

Background radiation results from the following.

▶ **Natural radiation** from radioactive elements in soil and rocks (e.g. granite) varies in different regions depending on the underlying rocks; other sources include buildings, food, and cosmic rays which penetrate the atmosphere.
▶ Additional small doses of radiation are received from medical **X-rays** of teeth and bones.
▶ Other human activity (the nuclear power industry, industrial uses of radioactive materials, and fallout from nuclear accidents and testing) contributes less than one per cent to the total.

3 Radioactive emissions

The table shows the properties of the three main types of radioactive emission.

Type of emission	Description	Penetrating power	Deflection by a magnetic field
Alpha particles (α)	Fast-moving helium nuclei (2 protons, 2 neutrons)	Absorbed by a few cm of air or stopped by a thin sheet of paper	Weakly deflected
Beta particles (β)	Fast-moving electrons	Easily pass through air or paper; stopped by thin sheets of metal	Deflected
Gamma rays (γ)	Short-wavelength electromagnetic radiation	Very penetrating; stopped by thick sheets of lead or thick concrete	Not deflected

H When radioactive atoms decay by *emitting particles* they change into other atoms.

Uranium-238 loses an α-particle to become thorium:

$$^{238}_{92}\text{U} \longrightarrow {}^{234}_{90}\text{Th} + {}^{4}_{2}\text{He}$$

Carbon-14 loses a β-particle to become nitrogen:

$$^{14}_{6}\text{C} \longrightarrow {}^{14}_{7}\text{N} + {}^{0}_{-1}\text{e}$$

4 Radioactive half-life

Different radioactive substances decay at different rates. A measure of the rate of decay of any one substance is called its **half-life**: the average time taken for the radioactivity of a sample to reduce by half. Half-lives can vary from less than 1 second to thousands of years. A graph of radioactive decay will always follow the same pattern.

Figure 13.1
The decay curve for radioactive materials

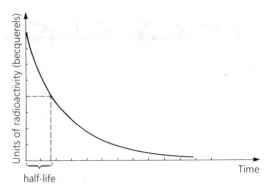

5 Effects of radiation on organisms

Absorption of nuclear radiation by living tissue causes the cells to become altered, damaged or even killed: the radiation **ionises** the molecules of the cells. It can cause genetic mutations or death of an organism. As a result safety precautions are required to prevent excessive exposure to radioactive materials. The effect of exposure depends on:

▶ the amount and type of radiation
▶ the length of exposure
▶ the number and type of cells exposed

Radiation can be beneficial: for example, gamma rays are used to kill cancerous body cells.

6 Uses of radioactivity

▶ Radioactive dating of archaeological specimens and rocks: the proportion of C-12 to C-14 is the same for all living things, but on death the amount of C-14 decreases and the amount left can be measured to date an item.
▶ Use of a gamma-emitting radioisotope as a **tracer** to detect malfunction of organs in the body.
▶ Monitoring the thickness of sheet metal or paper: as radiation passes through material it is absorbed, so the thicker the material the more radiation is absorbed.
▶ Tracing leaks in a water pipe by adding a radioisotope to the water and monitoring with a Geiger counter.
▶ Irradiation of food to destroy micro-organisms which cause moulds and toxins, thereby increasing its 'shelf life'.

Ⓗ 7 Fission

When bombarded by neutrons, some large unstable nuclei split into two smaller nuclei and release energy. This is called **nuclear fission** and is the process involved in nuclear reactors. On splitting, further neutrons are ejected which hit other nuclei and cause a **chain reaction**.

PRACTICE QUESTIONS

Question 1

In an experiment to study a radioisotope a teacher used a special detector to measure the radioactivity. The detector produced an electrical pulse when a radioactive particle entered it. The pulses were counted by an electrical counter.

(a) Name a suitable radioactivity detector.

....(1)

(b) The teacher first used the detector to measure the background radiation level. This was done by switching it on for one minute. The background count was found to be 24 counts/minute.

Suggest *two* sources of background radioactivity.

1. ....

....

2. ....

....(2)

(c) The teacher then placed the radioisotope close to the detector as shown in the diagram below. The radiation reaching the detector in one minute was measured.

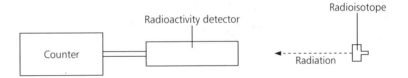

Then different materials were placed between the radioisotope and the detector. The radiation which reached the detector was measured each time.

During the experiments the teacher took great care not to bring the radioisotope near the hands or to point it at anyone. The results of the experiment are shown in the table below.

| | Radiation detected (counts/minute) | | | |
No material	Paper	Thin metal	Thick lead	Background count
895	460	24	24	24

(i) What type or types of radiation did this radioisotope emit?

....(1)

(ii) Explain the reasons for your answer.

....

....

....

....(3)

(d) Explain, as fully as you can, how the radioisotope could cause damage to your hand if you put your hand near it.

....

....

....

....(4)

(e) Radiation can also be used to treat cancer. A radioisotope that is often used is cobalt-60. This isotope has a proton number of 27 and a mass number of 60.
   (i) How many protons, neutrons and electrons does a cobalt-60 atom contain?

        number of protons   = ...

        number of neutrons = ...

        number of electrons = ...   (3)

   (ii) Radiation is used to treat cancerous growths. What does the radiation do?

        ....

        ....(1)

                                                              (Total marks 15)
                                                                        NEAB

Question 2
(a) The position of sodium, Na, is shown in the outline of the periodic table.

   (i) Sodium is a metal. Give *three* reasons why this is to be expected from its position in the periodic table.

        1. ....

        2. ....

        3. ....(3)

   (ii) Lithium is directly above sodium in the periodic table. Explain why sodium is more reactive than lithium.

        ....

        ....

        ....

        ....

        ....

        ....(3)

(b) The isotope of sodium $^{24}_{11}$Na is radioactive.

(i) The half-life of $^{24}_{11}$Na is 15 hours. Draw an accurate line graph on the grid below to show how the percentage of $^{24}_{11}$Na remaining in the sample changes with time.

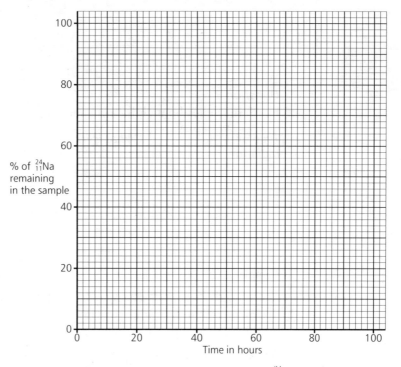

% of $^{24}_{11}$Na remaining in the sample

Time in hours

(2)

(ii) Use your line graph to find the amount of $^{24}_{11}$Na remaining from a 10 g sample after 40 hours. You must show how you find your answer.

....

....

....

....(3)

(c) The radiation from $^{24}_{11}$Na is mainly gamma (γ) rays. The other two types of ionising radiation are alpha (α) particles and beta (β) particles. State what these particles are.

Alpha (α) particles are...

....

Beta (β) particles are...

....(2)

(d) Study the information.

Isotope	Half-life	Main type of radiation
$^{220}_{86}$Rn	55 seconds	alpha (α)
$^{32}_{15}$P	14 days	beta (β)
$^{60}_{27}$Co	5 years	gamma (γ)
$^{238}_{94}$Pu	86 years	alpha (α)

(i) Heart pacemakers are powered using sealed isotopes. Which isotope would be the best to use? Give a reason for your choice.

....

....

....(2)

(ii) Radiation from cobalt-60 is used to kill cancer cells deep inside the human body. Radiation from phosphorus-32 is used for skin cancers. Explain why.

....

....

....

....(3)

(Total marks 18)

SEG

Question 3

(a) Finish the table about alpha, beta and gamma radiations.

Type of radiation	What is it?	What type of charge does it carry?
Alpha		
Beta	Electron	Negative
Gamma		

(4)

(b) Technetium-99m is a radioactive isotope which is often used by hospitals in the examination of patients. It emits only gamma rays; it has a half-life of 6 hours.

A doctor wishes to examine the action of a patient's heart. He injects a substance containing technetium-99m into the blood. It mixes with the blood. As the substance passes through the heart, the radiation from it is detected outside the patient's body. Measurements are made while 500 heart beats take place.

(i) Why does the doctor choose a gamma emitter with a half-life of 6 hours rather than one with a half-life of 6 minutes or 6 days?

....

....

....

....(4)

(ii) A sample of technetium-99m has a count-rate of 6400 counts per minute. After 24 hours the count-rate was calculated as 400 counts per minute. Explain how this calculation was made.

....

....

....(2)

(iii) When a single measurement of the count-rate was taken, it was 413 counts per minute. Suggest *two* reasons why the measured count-rate is different from the calculated value.

....

....(2)

(Total marks 12)

MEG

Solutions
The human body

Question 1
(a) Arrows in the correct place as shown. (2)

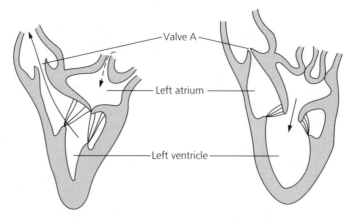

Examiner's note   The first diagram shows the ventricle contracting and valve A open to allow blood out (to the aorta); blood also flows into the left atrium (from the lungs). The second diagram shows the ventricle relaxing so blood flows from the atrium into the ventricle.

(b) Valve A prevents blood flowing back   (1)
     from the blood vessel into the atrium.   (1)   (2)

Examiner's note   The function of all valves is similar, to allow blood to flow one way so preventing blood flowing in the wrong direction.

(c) pulmonary vein   (1)

Examiner's note   Remember arteries carry blood *away* from the heart, the pulmonary vein is carrying blood from the lungs to the heart.

(d) The left ventricle pumps blood all round the body at high pressure.   (1)

Examiner's note   The left ventricle pumps oxygenated blood at high pressure to all parts of the body.

(Total marks 6)

Question 2
(a) There is less oxygen in the air breathed out because oxygen is used up by the body for the release of energy.   (1)
     There is more carbon dioxide in the air breathed out because carbon dioxide is produced in the body by respiration.   (1)   (2)

Examiner's note   Look at the data in the table to see how the level of oxygen drops from 20% to 16% and the level of carbon dioxide rises from 0.04% to 4% in air breathed out. State clearly how the levels change and then emphasise the essential process: *respiration*.

(b) Nitrogen gas is not used by the body.   (1)

Examiner's note   The levels are the same in both samples.

(c) lactic acid   (1)

Examiner's note   You are told in the question that the athlete is respiring *anaerobically* and so using up energy more quickly than oxygen can be supplied to the muscles. The glucose is converted to lactic acid (instead of carbon dioxide) which gives a burning sensation in the muscles.

(d) <u>When the athlete exercises vigorously the muscles</u> use up the available <u>oxygen</u> in the process of aerobic respiration.   (1)
<u>The buildup of an oxygen debt</u> means that <u>anaerobic respiration</u> has been used to release energy quickly so the athlete can continue with the exercise.   (1)   (2)

     Examiner's note   There seems to be a lot of explaining to do for 2 marks, however the underlined phrases above are given in the question. The oxygen debt is caused by not having enough oxygen to release sufficient energy for the vigorous activity.   (Total marks 6)

Question 3

(a) (i) The protein molecules are too large   (1)
     to pass through the capillary wall and capsule.   (1)
     Protein is needed to build new cells.   (1)   (3)

     Examiner's note   You are told in (i) that there is no protein present in the renal capsule and the table in (a) shows protein present in the blood in the renal artery. From your knowledge of proteins as large molecules it seems logical to suggest that proteins are too large to pass through the capillary walls. Also proteins would not be excreted from the body as they are needed for growth.

(ii) [A] Urea is poisonous.   (1)
     [B] The concentration of urea is higher as other substances have been reabsorbed back into the blood   (1)   (2)

     Examiner's note   Refer back to the table in (a) to see how the concentration of urea in the urine is higher than in the capsule. This is because water and other substances are reabsorbed from the tubule into the blood. The urea is toxic and is not reabsorbed.

(b) If the concentration of glucose was higher in the dialysis solution than the blood   (1)
then glucose would enter the blood   (1)
and cause hyperglycaemia (too much glucose).   (1)   (3)

or The glucose concentration must be the same to prevent glucose moving in or out of the blood   (1)
by diffusion.   (1)
This would change the glucose concentration in the blood.   (1)   (3)

     Examiner's note   Note: there are different ways of expressing the answer here. You could gain the 3 marks by explaining the effect of a higher concentration in the dialysis solution or write in more general terms the reason why the concentration must be the same.   (Total marks 8)

Question 4 – student's answer

(a) As tobacco consumption increased so did deaths from bronchitis.
     Examiner's note   Good.   (1/1)

(b) They like it.
     Examiner's note   Not enough for a mark – mention nicotine being addictive to gain the full 2 marks.   (0/2)

(c) (i) Artery has a thick muscular wall to withstand pressure.
     Examiner's note   Good, three clear points made – thick, muscular and withstand pressure.   (3/3)

  (ii) The smoker's artery is narrow so less blood flows to the heart.
     Examiner's note   Good – for a third mark you should state that pressure is increased.   (2/3)

(d) Less oxygen.
     Examiner's note   Good, but for the second mark state clearly that the haemoglobin will be unable to transport oxygen.   (1/2)

                                           Total score: 7/11

     Examiner's note   Good, but part (b) lost you 2 marks!

Solutions
Plants

ANSWERS TO PRACTICE QUESTIONS

Question 1

(a) carbon dioxide + water ⟶ glucose + oxygen

     (1)   (1)   (2)

Examiner's note   1 mark is allocated for the reactants, carbon dioxide and water, and 1 mark for the products. Alternative answers to glucose could be sugar or carbohydrate. If you had given a symbolic equation here you would still gain marks provided the formulae were correct!

(b) Tube A   (1)

because tubes B, C and D contained organisms which used up oxygen   (1)

during respiration.   (1)   (3)

Examiner's note   Read the information above and below the diagram. The test tubes were left in the dark for 24 hours and so no photosynthesis would take place. Tube A is the only tube which has no animals or plants using up the oxygen.

(c) Tube W   (1)

because woodlice and pondweed are both releasing carbon dioxide.   (1)

The black paper around tube W stops photosynthesis so no carbon dioxide being used up.   (1)   (3)

Examiner's note   Read the heading to the diagram and study the diagram carefully to obtain all the information you can. All the tubes were left in the light but notice that tubes W and Z have a black paper cover. Tube Z acts as a control to see if the level of carbon dioxide would change if there were no organisms present. In tube X the woodlice are respiring and giving out carbon dioxide but in tube W there are woodlice *and* plants giving out carbon dioxide. The plants in tube Y in the light would be using up carbon dioxide.   (Total marks 8)

Question 2

(a) Oxygen enters by diffusion.   (1)

(b) Water enters by osmosis:

water molecules move from an area of high concentration of water molecules   (1)

to an area of low concentration of water molecules   (1)

through a partially permeable membrane.   (1)   (3)

Examiner's note   You can see here why you need to learn names of processes and definitions. Use the diagram of the root hair cell to help you recall your notes on movement of substances in and out of cells. Remember osmosis is just a special type of diffusion which involves water molecules moving from high to low concentration.

(c) The sea water has a lower concentration of water molecules than the plants.   (1)

There is movement of water molecules from the roots into the water around the roots.   (1)   (2)

Examiner's note   An example of an application of osmosis.

(Total marks 6)

Question 3 – student's answer

(a) carbon dioxide + water + light energy $\longrightarrow$ sugar + oxygen

    Examiner's note   Good – no need for formulae as parts of the equation are given in words.

(2/2)

(b) The yellow areas have no chlorophyll so cannot produce sugar.

    Examiner's note   Yes, but you should state that 'chlorophyll is needed to absorb light energy for photosynthesis' to gain the other 2 marks.   (1/3)

(c) (i)   To grow strong roots.

    Examiner's note   Not enough for the mark – you need to say that nitrate is used to make proteins – growth is stated in the question!   (0/1)

   (ii) For photosynthesis.

    Examiner's note   Yes, but note that 2 marks are allocated – 'to make enzymes' is required for the second mark.   (1/2)

Total score: 4/8

    Examiner's note   Only half the marks for this question.

Solutions
Variation, inheritance and evolution

ANSWERS TO PRACTICE QUESTIONS

Question 1
(a) (i) 2 cells, 4 cells   (1)

   (ii) 12 chromosomes, 6 chromosomes   (1)   (2)

     Examiner's note   When cells divide to form new body cells, *two* cells are formed from each original cell. When gametes (egg or sperm) are produced, *four* cells are formed from each original cell. You are given information about the number of chromosomes, 12. The body cells all have the full number, 12, but the gametes have half this number, 6.

(b) Let H = symbol for the dominant gene,

   let h = symbol for recessive gene: (1)

   parents' genotypes Hh × hh   (1)

   gametes H and h, h and h   (1)

   Offspring genotypes are as shown in the table:

Gametes	h	h
H	Hh	Hh
h	hh	hh

                                        (1)

   Offspring phenotypes: Hh = Huntington's chorea; hh = normal.   (1)

   There would be a 50% chance of a child in this family inheriting Huntington's chorea.   (1)   (5)

     Examiner's note   Remember to state what your chosen letters stand for. The capital letter is usually for the dominant allele and the small letter for the recessive allele. In the information in (b) you are told one parent has a single dominant allele for Huntington's chorea (so will be Hh); the other parent carries two recessive alleles (hh). Follow through the sequence of stating the genotype of the parents (Hh and hh), the gametes (H and h) and the genotype of the offspring (Hh and hh). Use the checkerboard diagram to help you. Don't forget to state the 50% probability as a result of the 1:1 ratio of Hh to hh.

                                              (Total marks 7)

Question 2
(a) chemical substances   (1)

   transported in the blood   (1)

   produced by glands   (1)

   control target organs   (1)   (any 2 points)   (2)

     Examiner's note   Only two points need to be made for the 2 marks available. The information at the start of the question may help you to remember two facts about hormones in general. For example, you are told that insulin (a hormone) is made by the pancreas (an organ) and affects the concentration of glucose in the blood.

(b) (i)   By action of enzymes.   (1)

   (ii) [A] A clone is an exact copy   (1)

          formed from one parent.   (1)   (2)

       [B] Bacteria reproduce rapidly   (1)

          so a lot of insulin can be produced quickly.   (1)

> Bacteria produce identical genes   (1)
> and so produce identical insulin.   (1)   (any 3 points)   (3)
>> *Examiner's note*   The main point here is to give *reasons why* bacteria are suitable organisms, not just that they are 'simple organisms'.

(c) Genetically produced insulin is cheaper   (1)
and more readily available.   (1)   (2)
>> *Examiner's note*   Other answers you could have gained marks for include that genetically produced insulin is purer because it is all from the same gene, also there may be side effects associated with insulin extracted from animals. Any scientific suggestion is likely to gain marks.

(Total marks 10)

Question 3

(a) The farmer should select cows which give a high yield of milk   (1)
to breed the next generation of calves.   (1)
The cows could be given extra food supplements or hormones to increase growth.   (1)   (3)
>> *Examiner's note*   The photo (in the original examination paper) and the table are there as a stimulus to help you think about the question. To improve breeding stock most farmers would choose the best cattle to breed from.

(b) The farmer receives more money.   (1)
The milk could be made cheaper.   (1)   (2)
>> *Examiner's note*   Any two sensible suggestions would gain you the marks.

(Total marks 5)

Question 4 – student's answer

(a) (i) Decide what characteristics are wanted, then choose those animals which show those features and breed from them.
>> *Examiner's note*   Well done, you have made three points here – decide characteristics, choose animals, breed.   (3/3)

 (ii) Resistance to disease and milk yield.
>> *Examiner's note*   Resistance to disease applies but milk yield does not – note that the question refers to 'wheat crop'.   (1/2)

(b) (i) Hh
>> *Examiner's note*   Good – one allele from each parent.   (1/1)

 (ii) All F_1 are tall.
>> *Examiner's note*   Good – the F_1 inherit the dominant allele for tallness and the recessive allele but the phenotype shows the dominant feature. Use a checkerboard sketch to write the genotypes HH, Hh, Hh, hh – those with a H will be tall.   (1/1)

 (iii) 3/4 tall to 1/4 short.
>> *Examiner's note*   Good enough for one mark but the question asks you to 'explain'.   (1/2)

(c) (i) Insert DNA into the cereal and breed from those.
>> *Examiner's note*   Good but add that the DNA is on the gene which has the nitrogen-fixing ability for 2 more marks.   (1/3)

 (ii) A mutant could be produced which might breed with normal organisms and produce a harmful organism.
>> *Examiner's note*   Good, you have made three clear points – production of a mutant, breeding, producing a harmful organism.   (3/3)

Total score: 11/15

>> *Examiner's note*   Well done.

Solutions
Ecology

ANSWERS TO PRACTICE QUESTIONS

Question 1

(a) (i) The rabbit population has stopped increasing.   (1)
Examiner's note   The graph levels off at point A, meaning no increase in numbers.

(ii) The food (or water) supply may have become limited.   (1)
A change in environmental conditions may have limited breeding.   (1)   (2)

(b) (i) The predators eat the rabbits so the rabbit population falls.   (1)
Examiner's note   This is testing that you know what a 'predator' is.

(ii) As there are fewer rabbits there is less food for the predators   (1)
so the predator population decreases.   (1)   (2)
Examiner's note   Assuming the predators only eat rabbits, when there are less rabbits there will be less predators.

(iii) The numbers of rabbits and predators will continue the pattern.   (1)
The number of rabbits increases so the number of predators increases.   (1)
This causes a fall in the number of rabbits so the number of predators decreases.   (1)   (3)
Examiner's note   It is logical to assume that the pattern will continue but you cannot gain 3 marks for just writing one fact, so state the obvious about each population rising and falling to show the examiner you really understand what happens!

(Total marks 9)

Question 2

(a) leaf litter $\longrightarrow$ earthworms $\longrightarrow$ beetles $\longrightarrow$ shrews   (2)
Examiner's note   Start with one organism from the bottom of the food web and then select one organism from each level; 1 mark is allocated for the correct organisms, 1 mark for the arrows pointing to the right, from the producer to the consumer.

(b) If there are less weasels then fewer small birds would be eaten;   (1)
the population of small birds would rise;   (1)
more small birds would eat the moths;   (1)
the population of the moths would decrease.   (1)   (4)
Examiner's note   Note: the question asks about the populations of small birds *and* moths. Try to make two clear statements about each to gain full marks.

(c) (i)   voles/small birds/shrews   (1)
Examiner's note   This diagram links to the diagram in (a). Look across from X and count to the third level on the food web to find your answer.

(ii) On the pyramid of numbers, level Y shows the oak trees:
these are large organisms   (1)
and so there are few of them   (1)
but they have a large biomass.   (1)   (3)

Examiner's note   The pyramid of numbers shows only a few organisms at level Y. Check across to the diagram in (a) to see what these organisms are. The pyramid of biomass shows a large amount of biomass at level Y. Use the vocabulary in the diagrams for (c) to help you in your answer.

(d) (i)   The leaf litter was broken down (decayed)   (1)
     by the microbes or earthworms (bacteria/fungi).   (1)   (2)
     Examiner's note   Read the information about the graph and then notice how the line on the graph dips down. Think about the woodland and about nutrient cycles.

(ii)   March, because
     the microbes or earthworms may be more active   (1)
     when the temperatures are higher   (1)   (2)
     Examiner's note   There is no mark for March, but 2 marks for explanation. Think about what you know about how temperatures often rise as spring comes. There are no definitive answers here; plausible scientific suggestions will gain marks.

(iii) Microbes (bacteria, fungi, decomposers)   (1)
     break down proteins into ammonium compounds.   (1)
     Nitrifying bacteria   (1)
     convert ammonium into nitrates   (1)
     which are absorbed by roots   (1)
     and combined with sugars to produce protein.   (1)   (6)
     Examiner's note   This answer relies on your understanding of the nitrogen cycle but use the information in question (iii) to help you in remembering the sequence. Note you would not gain marks for stating that these were nitrogen-fixing bacteria or denitrifying bacteria.

           (Total marks 20)

Question 3
(a) (i)   1875 kJ (lost in faeces and urine) + 1000 kJ (respiration) = 2875 kJ (total lost by cow)
     3000 kJ (taken up by cow) − 2875 kJ (lost by cow) = 225 kJ (used for growth)   (1)

$$\frac{225 \times 100\%}{1\,000\,000} + 0.0225\% \quad (1)$$ (2)

     Examiner's note   This may appear complicated but the figures are all on the diagram. Look at how much energy is taken up by the cow (3000 kJ) and how much it loses in respiration (1000 kJ) and faeces/urine (1875 kJ). The amount left is what is used for growth (225 kJ). Work this out as a percentage of the 1 000 000 kJ of energy originally falling on the grass as shown above.

(ii)   The diagram shows energy lost from a cow by respiration and excretion;   (1)
     at each trophic level of the food chain energy is lost.   (1)   (2)

(b) (i)   Radiant energy from Sun passes through atmosphere;   (1)
     some is absorbed by Earth, some is radiated back   (1)
     but is trapped by 'greenhouse' gases   (1)
     and radiated back to Earth.   (1)   (4)
     Examiner's note   You are given a clue in the wording of (b) that *gases in the atmosphere trap energy*; remember what you can about greenhouses and how they feel warmer than outside air because of heat trapped inside, and you are on your way to scoring 2 or 3 marks!

(ii)   Increase in greenhouse gases may lead to global warming:
     ice caps could melt and cause rise in sea levels;   (1)
     greater extremes of climate could result.   (1)   (2)

Examiner's note   Think logically about the effect on the polar regions of the Earth becoming warmer.

(Total marks 9)

Question 4

(a) 35–40 years   (1)

Examiner's note   The population was 2500 million in 1950. The question asks how many years until the population doubled (to 5000 million). Look along from the 5000 mark and use your ruler to help you draw a vertical line down to the horizontal axis at about 1985, 35 years on. Hint, one small square on the x-axis = 5 years.

(b) food production must be increased   (1)

more fertilisers   (1)

more pesticides   (1)

increased use of non-renewable energy sources such as fossil fuels   (1)

greater pollution, for example carbon dioxide   (1)

increased risk of global warming   (1)

increased use of nuclear fuels/disposal problems of nuclear waste   (1)

greater deforestation/desertification   (1)   (any 6 points)   (6)

Examiner's note   In an account like this choose scientific points related to population increase; try to link two or three statements together, for example increased use of fossil fuels leads to increase in carbon dioxide levels, etc. If you are stuck for ideas, think about what *your* needs are – food, housing, electricity, transport, etc., and how these needs might cause problems if 6000 million people wanted them.

(Total marks 7)

Question 5 – student's answer

(a) 1. Photosynthesis

2. Transpiration

3. Decomposition

4. Burning

5. Feeding

Examiner's note   For this question you do not use *all* the words given, however, the answer in box 2 should be 'respiration' not transpiration. (4/5)

(b) (i) To break down dead animals and plants to release nutrients.

Examiner's note   Yes, but add 'to release carbon dioxide' for the second mark.   (1/2)

(ii) Bacteria

Examiner's note   Yes, but you are asked for two so add 'fungi' for the second mark.   (1/3)

Total score: 6/9

5 Solutions
Periodic table, atomic structure and bonding

ANSWERS TO PRACTICE QUESTIONS

Question 1

(a) (i) group 1, the alkali metals   (1)
   Examiner's note   By referring to the periodic table you can see the
   position of rubidium in the same group as potassium and sodium.

   (ii) rubidium hydroxide   (1)
         hydrogen   (1)   (2)
   Examiner's note   The pattern of reaction with water is the same for all the
   alkali metals (M):

   $$2M + 2H_2O \longrightarrow 2MOH + H_2$$

   Examiner's note   Remember you are asked to state *two* products.

   (iii) The metal fizzes   (1)
         and flames.   (1)   (2)
   Examiner's note   Use your knowledge of the reactive nature of the alkali
   metals to state *two* observations. Reactivity increases down the group so
   you can predict that rubidium will react violently with water.

(b) (i) hydrochloric acid   (1)
   Examiner's note   You are asked to name a liquid so any named acid will
   gain the mark.

   (ii) magnesium iodide   (1)
         hydrogen   (1)   (2)
   Examiner's note   The magnesium displaces the hydrogen and forms a
   metal halide.

   (iii) Bubbles appear   (1)
         and the magnesium dissolves.   (1)   (2)
   Examiner's note   Remember the reaction between magnesium and
   hydrochloric acid.

(c) (i)   The indicator would show a red/orange colour, showing acidity.   (1)

   (ii) There would be fizzing   (1)
         and the sodium carbonate dissolves   (1)   (2)

   (iii) carbon dioxide/water/sodium selenate   (1)
   Examiner's note   Use the periodic table to find another familiar element,
   sulphur, which is in the same group as selenium then apply your knowledge
   of how sulphur and sulphuric acid behave to this question.

(Total marks 14)

Question 2

(a) $2Na + Cl_2 \longrightarrow 2NaCl$ (1)
   Examiner's note   You are given $Na + Cl_2 \longrightarrow NaCl$ in the
   question. NaCl is the formula for sodium chloride. There are 2 Cl on the left
   so there must be 2 Cl on the right. The only way to obtain this is to have 2
   NaCl on the right. To balance the equation there must be 2 Na on the left.

(b) (i)   The number of electrons in the shells of the sodium atom should be
2, 8, 1.   (1)
The number of electrons in the shells of the chlorine atom should be
2, 8, 7.   (1)   (2)
Examiner's note   Use a data book (provided in the exam) to look up the
atomic numbers of sodium (11) and chlorine (17). Remember that there are
2 electrons in the first shell (already shown) and a maximum of 8 in the
outer shells.

(ii)   The atom loses   (1)   one electron.   (1)   (2)
Examiner's note   The loss of an electron makes the sodium atom positively
charged and very reactive.

(c) (i)   1. chlorine   (1)   2. hydrogen   (1)   (2)
Examiner's note   1. The chlorine ions are attracted to the positive
electrode (the anode) where they lose electrons and change back into
chlorine atoms. The atoms join in pairs to form the gas.
2. The hydrogen ions are attracted to the negative electrode (the cathode)
where they gain electrons and change into hydrogen atoms which join in
pairs to form the gas.

(ii)   in the manufacture of margarine   (1)

(iii) sodium hydroxide   (1)
Examiner's note Na^+ is the formula for the sodium ion, OH^- is the
hydroxide ion; the chemical formed is sodium hydroxide.

(d) (i)   KCl   (1)
Examiner's note   Use your data book to remind you of the symbol for
potassium. It is a group 1 metal and it has one electron in the outer shell to
bond with chlorine which has one space to fill in the outer shell.

(ii)   Sodium and potassium are group 1 metals: both have one electron in
their outer shell.   (1)

(e) (i)   Fluorine gains an electron more easily than chlorine: (1)
it is a smaller atom than chlorine   (1)
so its outer shell is closer to the positive nucleus which has a strong
pulling power.   (1)   (3)
Examiner's note   Use the copy of the periodic table in your data book to
help remind you of the relative positions and atomic numbers of fluorine
(9) and chlorine (17). The ease with which the atoms form ions depends on
the number of electron shells. The larger the atom the further away the
outer shell, so the less influence the nucleus will have.

(ii)   The outer electron shells are full   (1)   so the atoms are stable   (1)
and have no tendency to lose or gain electrons.   (1)   (3)

(iii) Radon is likely to react.   (1)
It is in a lower group than xenon which does not react   (1)
and reactivity increases down the group.   (1)   (3)
Examiner's note   Read the information again at the start of question (e).
You are told that fluorine does not react with argon but will react with
xenon. Use the periodic table to look at the positions of argon, xenon and
radon. Radon is below xenon and so is likely to react.

(Total marks 20)

Question 3

(a) (i)   6 protons ⊕   (1)   8 neutrons ●   (1)
6 (2 + 4) electrons ⊖   (1)   (3)

Examiner's note Carbon-14 has the same number of protons and electrons (6) as carbon-12 because they are isotopes. Carbon-14, however, has a mass number of 14 so it has 8 neutrons (14 − 6).

(ii) $\oplus$ proton (1)   ● neutron (1) $\ominus$ electron (1)   (3)
Examiner's note Protons are positively charged; neutrons are neutral; electrons are negatively charged.

(iii) The nucleus (1)
releases alpha, beta and gamma rays. (1)   (2)
Examiner's note Remember it is the *nucleus* and not the atom that releases radioactivity.

(iv) Atoms of the same element (1)
with different mass number (different number of neutrons) (1)
but same atomic number (same number of protons) (1)   (3)
Examiner's note You may find help by reading the information given in (a) and your answer to (a) (i).

(b) (i) Diamond is a macromolecule (giant molecule); (1)
every carbon atom in diamond is strongly linked (bonded) to four carbon atoms. (1)   (2)
Examiner's note Diamond forms a giant structure with a 3D arrangement of molecules.

(ii) Every carbon atom in graphite is bonded to three carbon atoms in layers; (1)
the forces (bonds) holding the layers together are weak. (1)   (2)
Examiner's note Graphite is strongly bonded but in layers; each layer is a giant molecule but the weak bonds between the layers allow the layers to slide over each other, so helping your pencil to mark the page!

(iii) Both are giant structures.   (1)

(c) Graphite (1)
because it has free electrons. (1)   (2)
Examiner's note Giant molecules do not normally conduct electricity but graphite is the exception.

(d) (i) A typical metal oxide has a high melting point.   (1)
(ii) A typical metal oxide is a basic oxide.   (1)
Examiner's note Metals (such as group 1, alkali metals) form basic oxides which dissolve in water to produce alkaline solutions.

(Total marks 20)

Question 4 – student's answer

(a) Each row across is an electron shell. The shell fills up from 1 to 8 electrons as the elements go across the table, the atomic number increases by one.
Examiner's note Good, try to make three logical points about the 'electronic structure' asked for in the question.   (3/3)

(b) Sodium has one electron in its outer shell. When it becomes an ion it loses the electron and becomes positively charged.
Examiner's note Great, but you need to write about chlorine gaining an electron for the second mark.   (1/2)

Total score: 4/5

Solutions
Useful products from oil and metals

ANSWERS TO PRACTICE QUESTIONS

Question 1

(a) A compound made only from carbon and hydrogen. (1)

Examiner's note Use the diagram to help you see that there are only two elements in hydrocarbons, C and H. Identify the names of the elements from the periodic table in a data book.

(b) C_5H_{12} (1)

Examiner's note In the diagram count the number of carbon atoms, 5, and then count the number of hydrogen atoms, 12. Remember to write the number of atoms as subscript (below the line).

(c) **In fractional distillation** crude oil is heated and the fractions evaporate; (1) the fractions are condensed (1) at different temperatures. (1) Each fraction contains hydrocarbons with similar chain length (similar number of carbon atoms). (1)
In cracking the large hydrocarbons are broken down into shorter molecules. (1) (these points or similar) (5)

Examiner's note Notice how no marks are awarded for the terms 'fractional distillation' and 'cracking' as these are used in the question. You can still use them to divide your answer into two sections. Try to include at least 4–5 scientific facts in your answer to gain the marks. The diagram may help you with the idea of breaking down long chains into shorter chains.

(d) It has some double bonds. (1)

Examiner's note When carbon atoms are linked by a double bond they are described as 'unsaturated'. 'Saturated' hydrocarbons have single carbon–carbon bonds.

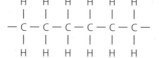

(e) Correct linkage shown as here. (2)

Examiner's note One of the carbon double bonds is used to link to the next carbon atom.

(f) (i) It does not react with the food. (1)

Examiner's note Although there are many possible answers (cheap, light, good insulation), try to use one that is as scientific as possible.

   (ii) When thermosetting plastics are heated, strong cross links form between adjacent chains of molecules. (1)
   These bonds are not broken by reheating. (1) (2)

Examiner's note Attempt this even if you do not know the answer. The word 'thermosetting' may give you a clue to the idea that there are strong bonds in the plastic. (Total marks 13)

Question 2

(a) (i) As the density of the alkanes increases, so the energy released by combustion increases. (1)

Examiner's note On the table look at how the numbers for density get higher as well as the energy released by combustion. This is a pattern or trend.

   (ii) between 0.59 and 0.61 g/cm³ (1)

Examiner's note It's quite OK to give a range of figures when asked to 'suggest' a value; anywhere above the density of propane and below that of pentane fits the pattern.

(iii) For each alkane the number of carbon atoms increases by 1   (1)
   and the number of hydrogen atoms increases by 2.   (1)   (2)
   Examiner's note   Look at the formula given in column 2 of the table to work out the answer. You could also say that CH_2 is added each time.

(iv) C_6H_{14} (1)
   Examiner's note   Hexane follows the trend so has 1 more carbon and 2 more hydrogen atoms than pentane.

(b) (i) $3550 \pm 50 \, kJ/mol$ (1)
   Examiner's note   Look at the table in (a) to see how many carbon atoms are in pentane (5). Use a ruler to see where the vertical from 5 carbon atoms on the x-axis crosses the line. It is just less than 3550.

(ii) oxygen   (1)

(iii) carbon dioxide   (1)   water   (1)   (2)
   Examiner's note   When hydrocarbons burn they form carbon dioxide and water.

(iv) carbon monoxide   (1)
   Examiner's note   Incomplete combustion takes place in a limited supply of air.

(v) More oxygen is needed for complete combustion to take place.   (1)
   Examiner's note   More carbon atoms means more oxygen is needed. Try to remember terms like 'complete'/'incomplete' combustion to ensure you gain full marks.   (Total marks 11)

Question 3

(a) The ions cannot flow in solid aluminium oxide.   (1)
   Examiner's note   Electrolysis is carried out on molten aluminium oxide to allow the ions to move to the electrodes.

(b) Aluminium ions (Al^{3+}) move to the cathode (negative)   (1)
   where they gain electrons and become aluminium atoms.   (1)
   $$Al^{3+} + 3e^- \longrightarrow Al \qquad (1)$$ (3)
   Examiner's note   Look at the information given in the question: you are told the formula for aluminium ions; to change the ions into aluminium atoms, 3 electrons are required.

(c) At the anode, oxygen ions are changed into oxygen gas.   (1)
   The carbon and oxygen react at high temperatures to form carbon dioxide gas.   (1)   (2)
   Examiner's note   You are given the information that oxygen ions are produced; it is logical to assume that the oxygen formed reacts with the carbon to form CO_2.   (Total marks 6)

Question 4 – student's answer

(a) (i)   It occurs naturally.
   Examiner's note   Good – it's not combined with oxygen.   (1/1)

(ii) It's very hard.
   Examiner's note   Yes, but you should emphasise that it is harder than rock.   (1/1)

(b) (i)   Reduction – reduction is the removal of oxygen by carbon.
   Examiner's note   Yes – eliminate the others – *carbon* reduces the iron oxide. Your explanation is excellent.   (2/2)

(ii) Iron oxide + air → iron + carbon dioxide
   Examiner's note   *Air* does not reduce the iron oxide, you need 'carbon' here. Note that the left side of the equation must be correct for 1 mark.   (1/2)

(iii) Helps the furnace to get hot.
   Examiner's note   Yes, but it is also needed to make the coke burn and form carbon dioxide.   (1/2)

(c) Gold is rare so it is expensive. It is cheap to extract iron but aluminium needs electricity which costs a lot.
   Examiner's note   Excellent – three clear points, one about each metal. A good answer.   (3/3)

Total score: 9/11

Solutions
Chemical reactions

Question 1

(a) Marks given on this graph:
    sensible scale chosen   (1)
    axes both labelled   (1)
    all points correctly plotted   (1)
    smooth curve drawn   (1)   (4)

    Examiner's note The examiner will look for the above marking points when marking your graph. In the exam an area of graph paper will be provided; its size is usually chosen to fit the data so make full use of the graph paper when selecting your scale. The time goes on the horizontal axis: 10 small squares per minute would probably be suitable. The gas given off goes on the vertical axis: one small square per cm^3 of gas would probably be suitable. You are asked in the question to join the points with a smooth curve and label this line X.

(b) The curve would have a less steep gradient;   (1)
    maximum volume $25\,cm^3$.   (1)   (2)

    Examiner's note Read the introduction to the question again. You are told that manganese dioxide speeds up this reaction so less time is taken and your sketch line must be less steep than line X. Now look carefully at the volume of hydrogen peroxide used in both experiments. Your line X shows the results for $50\,cm^3$ of hydrogen peroxide, but this second experiment uses only $25\,cm^3$. Your sketch line can only reach a maximum volume of $25\,cm^3$ of gas.

(c) There are less H_2O_2 particles available as they are broken down during the reaction,   (1)
    so less chance of collisions   (1)
    when a catalyst is used.   (1)   (3)

    Examiner's note The question tells you that hydrogen peroxide decomposes. This may help you to think about what happens to the reacting particles during the experiment. As the particles decompose there are less of them for releasing the gas.

(d) More energy supplied to the moving particles   (1)
    increases the rate of collisions between reactants   (1)
    and makes more energy available to make and break bonds.   (1)   (3)

    Examiner's note Increasing the temperature makes the particles move more quickly and collide more often.

(e) (i) Exothermic;   (1)
         65.1 kJ of energy released.   (1)   (2)

        Examiner's note The step shape of the diagram and the direction of the arrow should help you to realise that energy is being given out. The amount of energy is given next to the arrow.

    (ii) More energy   (1)
         is given out in forming new bonds   (1)
         than in breaking bonds.   (1)   (3)

        Examiner's note Read carefully the description given in (e) of what the reactants are and relate this to the diagram. The making of the new bonds in the calcium hydroxide uses less energy than is needed to break the bonds in the calcium oxide and the water.   (Total marks 17)

Question 2

(a) (i) hydrogen (1)

(ii) oxygen (1)

Examiner's note You are given two clues here to help you: the electrolysis diagram, and the tests for the gases released. Remember: hydrogen 'pops' (HP), oxygen relights (OR).

(iii) The molecular formula for water is H_2O (1)
so water contains twice as many hydrogen molecules as oxygen. (1) (2)

Examiner's note Write down the formula for water and you have your clue to the answer.

(b) There would be a pink-brown deposit at the negative electrode. (1)

Examiner's note Electrolysis of copper sulphate solution results in positively charged copper ions being attracted to the negative electrode and deposited as pink-brown copper; note you are asked for a *colour change*.

(Total marks 5)

Question 3

(a) The colour of the solution will change from blue to green. (1)
Solid copper will be formed. (1) (2)

Examiner's note You are told in the information that chromium forms green compounds. It will displace the copper from solution. This will precipitate as a solid and have a characteristic pink-brown colour.

(b) $2Cr + 6HCl \longrightarrow 2CrCl_3 + 3H_2$ (2)

Examiner's note You will obtain 1 mark for the correct formulae, even if the equation is unbalanced.

(c) carbon; red heat (1)

Examiner's note Carbon will reduce chromium(III) oxide at very high temperatures.

(d) (i) The bumper will go rusty. (1)
The iron reacts with oxygen in the air. (1) (2)

Examiner's note The reason car bumpers are coated with chromium is to prevent the iron from rusting.

(ii) $Cr^{3+} + 3e^- \longrightarrow Cr$ (1)

Examiner's note The chromium ion needs 3 electrons to form the chromium atom.

(Total marks 8)

Question 4 – student's answer

(a) It speeds up the process.

Examiner's note You should also use the word catalyst here. (1/1)

(b) (i) It goes down.

Examiner's note Yes, it decreases across the table. (1/1)

(ii) It goes up.

Examiner's note Yes, it increases down the table. (1/1)

(c) More energy given to the particles so they move faster and hit each other more often.

Examiner's note Good, there are three clear points – more energy, move faster, collisions occur more often. (3/3)

(d) It goes more quickly.

Examiner's note Good. (1/1)

Total score: 7/7

Examiner's note Full marks – excellent!

8

Solutions
The solar system; the Earth's geology and atmosphere

ANSWERS TO PRACTICE QUESTIONS

Question 1

(a) (i) Neptune (1)

Examiner's note   Neptune is the planet furthest away from the Sun, 4469 million km.

(ii) Venus (1)

Examiner's note   Earth is 149 million km from the Sun and Venus is 108 million km from the Sun so Venus is the closest planet to Earth.

(iii) The large planets have a low density. (1)

Examiner's note   The planets which have a large radius, such as Jupiter, Uranus and Neptune, all have low densities.

(iv) The high density planets are nearer the Sun

or density decreases further away from the Sun. (1)

Examiner's note   The planets with the highest densities, Mercury, Venus, Earth, and Mars, are all nearer the Sun.

(b) (i) Large gas clouds shrink due to their own gravity;   (1)
the core becomes very hot   (1)
and nuclear reactions begin.   (1) (3)

Examiner's note   You are given a clue in (i) that stars form from large gas clouds.

(ii) red giant   (1)
white dwarf   (1) (2)

Examiner's note   You are given these names in a list of four to choose from. The white dwarf forms when the red giant collapses. Eventually all nuclear reactions stop and a dark body is formed.

(iii) Nuclear fusion;   (1)
small nuclei combine to form larger ones;   (1)
hydrogen is converted to helium and energy is released.   (1) (3)

(c) (i) 580–595 nm (1)

Examiner's note   There is a lot of information here in the table and on the graph but it is much less complicated than it looks! Use the graph to see at which wavelength sodium absorbs light: the graph shows a marked dip at about 590 nm.

(ii) yellow/orange (1)

Examiner's note   Look on the table in (c) to find out what colour light has a wavelength of about 590 nm.

(d) (i) It has shifted towards a longer wavelength ('red shift'). (1)

Examiner's note   The graph on the left shows the fingerprint of the element measured on Earth. The second graph shows the fingerprint measured in the light from a distant star. Look how the 'fingerprint' line on the second graph has moved or shifted towards the red end of the spectrum.

(ii) Red shift of light from stars in distant galaxies shows galaxies are moving apart.   (1)
Red shift greater the further away the galaxy, showing more distant galaxies are moving apart faster.   (1)

These observations confirm that the Universe is expanding as postulated by the big bang theory. (1)

Observation of 'background' microwave radiation is further evidence for the origin of the Universe in an explosion. (1) (4)

Examiner's note This may seem quite difficult to explain but make an attempt to scientifically explain the evidence for the big bang. Even if you only gain 1 or 2 marks here it could make all the difference!

(Total marks 19)

Question 2

(a) (i) Magma forming new rocks. (1)

Examiner's note Where the ocean plates are spreading and pulling apart from each other magma rises from below the surface and forms new rocks. Another possibility is that volcanoes may occur.

(ii) The ocean plates pull apart; (1)
earthquakes sometimes occur at the edges. (1) (2)

Examiner's note This is about plate tectonics: the plates are interacting by moving in relation to each other as a result of convection currents.

(b) Theory of plate tectonics (continental drift); (1)
plates floating on mantle have moved apart; (1)
shape of land masses has changed. (1)
Plates will move further apart in future, land masses may change shape. (1) (4)

Examiner's note Look carefully at the diagrams you are given and state the obvious that the shape of the land masses has changed. Use the information from (a) about convection currents in the mantle and the diagram of the plates to help you with ideas and correct terminology.

(Total marks 7)

Question 3 – student's answer

(a)

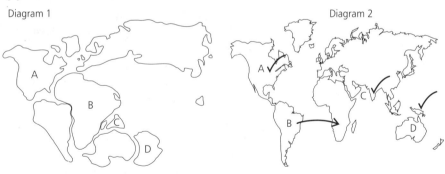

Diagram 1   Diagram 2

Examiner's note B should be marked on Africa. (1/2)

(b) 1. The shapes look like they fit together.
2.

Examiner's note Good, try 'similar rock formations' for the second point. (1/2)

(c) Convection currents in the mantle.

Examiner's note Yes – the heat is produced by radioactive reactions. (2/3)

(d) The ocean plate is denser and is pushed down. Plate D will be pushed up – possibly earthquakes and volcanoes.

Examiner's note Excellent – you have given a good description as asked for in the question.

(4/4)

Total score: 8/11

Solutions
Electricity and magnetism

ANSWERS TO PRACTICE QUESTIONS

Question 1

(a) (i) an electric fire   (1)
   (ii) a loudspeaker   (1)
   (iii) a spin drier   (1)   (3)
   Examiner's note   Think about household electrical devices to help you
   answer this question.

(b) (i)   The brown wire should be connected to the live pin, C.
       The blue wire should be connected to the neutral pin, A.   (1)
       Examiner's note   You need to learn the correct way of wiring a plug. It
       could save your life!

   (ii) The green/yellow wire is connected to the earth pin so the electricity
        runs to earth if there is a fault.   (1)
        The lawn mower has a plastic casing which acts as an insulator.   (1) (2)
        Examiner's note   The diagram in (b) shows that the lawn mower has a
        plastic body which insulates the user against a fault in the electric circuit.
        The electricity cannot reach the user.

(c) (i) $\text{current} = \dfrac{\text{power}}{\text{voltage}} = \dfrac{1250}{240}$ (1)

                            $= 5.2\,\text{A}$ (1)   (2)
       Examiner's note   You need to have learnt the formula given above. Insert
       the figures you are given in (c) into the formula. Don't forget the unit of
       the answer! If your result looks totally wrong try again; the answer should
       only be a few amps otherwise the lawn mower would overheat.

   (ii) 13 A   (1)
        Examiner's note   You are given four fuses to choose from; go for the one
        which is higher than the actual current value. The 13 A fuse would take a
        little more current before it broke the circuit.

(d) (i) iron   (1)
   (ii) A magnetic field is produced in the core.   (1)
   (iii) A current is induced in the secondary coil.   (1)
        Examiner's note   Look carefully at the diagram to see that there is no
        electrical connection between the primary and secondary coil. Current is
        induced in the secondary coil.

                                                          (Total marks 12)

Question 2

(a) (i) $\text{resistance} = \dfrac{\text{voltage}}{\text{current}} = \dfrac{4}{1.25}$ (1)

                            $= 3.2\,(\Omega)$ (1)   (2)
       Examiner's note   To gain both marks here show how you arrived at the
       answer by stating the formula and inserting the figures you are given into
       the formula. If you only state '3.2' without showing your working you only
       gain 1 mark. You are given the unit in the space for your answer.

   (ii) $\text{current} = \dfrac{\text{voltage}}{\text{resistance}} = \dfrac{12}{3.2}$ (1)

                            $= 3.75\,(\text{A})$ (1)   (2)

> *Examiner's note*   To gain maximum marks state the formula and insert the 12 V you are given in the question and your answer (3.2 Ω) from (i). The unit is given.

(b) (i)   The resistance increased   (1)
>   as the temperature increased.   (1)   (2)

> *Examiner's note*   State how the resistance changed: look at the graph to see that it increased due to an increase in the current which caused an increase in temperature.

   (ii)   resistance = 2 Ω   (1)
>   voltage = resistance × current = 2 × 0.5   (1)
>   = 1 (V)   (1)   (3)

> *Examiner's note*   Read on the graph the resistance when the current is 0.5 A. State the formula: voltage = resistance × current, and insert into the formula the reading from the graph (2 Ω) and 0.5 A. The unit is given.

  (iii) power = voltage × current = 1 × 0.5   (1)
>   = 0.5 W   (1)   (2)

> *Examiner's note*   State the formula and insert into the formula the figure of 1 V from (ii) and the 0.5 A given in the question. You need to state here the unit of power W (watts).   (Total marks 11)

Question 3

(a) By rubbing the perspex rod with a piece of cloth.   (1)

(b) The cloth removes   (1)
     electrons from the rod.   (1)   (2)

(c) A buildup of electrostatic charge on the tanker could cause a spark to be produced,   (1)
     which could ignite the fumes from the petrol and cause an explosion.   (1)   (2)

                                          (Total marks 5)

Question 4

(a) 1.   Add an extra cell.   (1)
     2.   Increase the strength of the magnet.   (1)   (2)

(b) (i)   There is relative movement between a magnetic field and a conducting coil   (1)
         so a voltage is induced in the coil   (1)
         and a current flows through the ammeter.   (1)   (3)
   (ii) By moving the matnet more quickly into the coil.   (1)

                                          (Total marks 6)

Question 5 – student's answer

(a) LDR
> *Examiner's note*   Yes – a light dependent resistor.   (1/1)

(b) As more paper is placed between the lamp and the LDR so less light passes through, resistance of LDR decreases so more current.
> *Examiner's note*   One mark for the first part (more paper therefore less light) however the second part of the answer is wrong. The resistance *increases* so *less* current – see how the graph goes down showing the current *decreases*.   (1/3)

(c) About 0.12 mm
> *Examiner's note*   Good – use the ruler to help you read from the graph. (1/1)

(d) $R = \dfrac{\text{Voltage}}{\text{Current}} = \dfrac{5}{40} = 0.125\ \Omega$

> *Examiner's note*   In your calculation 40 represents milliamps. You need to change the 40 milliamps to 0.04 amps. The answer is 125 Ω for the full 4 marks. However 3 marks for correct formula and process.   (3/4)

                                          Total score: 6/9

10

Solutions
Energy transfer and energy resources

ANSWERS TO PRACTICE QUESTIONS

Question 1

(a) Water is heated when coal is burned.   (1)
High-pressure steam turns turbines   (1)
which drive the rotor of a generator.   (1)   (3)

> *Examiner's note*   You are given clues to the answer in the wording of
> (a) 'drive generators' and also in (b) 'driving turbines'.

(b) No burning (combustion);   (1)
turbine is driven directly by movement of water.   (1)   (2)

> *Examiner's note*   The diagram shows you the level of high and low tides
> and the flow of water to help you work out what happens.

(c) *Advantages of coal:*   fairly cheap and gives a high energy output   (1)
  readily available   (1)
  Advantages of tidal: renewable energy source   (1)
  no pollution   (1)
  Disadvantages of coal: non-renewable energy source   (1)
  can cause pollution, e.g. acid rain   (1)
  Disadvantages of tidal: unsightly   (1)
  high cost of development   (1)   (8)

> *Examiner's note*   To make sure you gain all the marks here, divide your
> answer into four sections: advantages of (i) coal, (ii) tidal; disadvantages of
> (i) coal, (ii) tidal; state two facts for each to gain 2 marks per section,
> total 8 marks.

(Total marks 13)

Question 2

(a) coal   (1)

> *Examiner's note*   Any non-renewable source will do (oil, gas, uranium);
> you are given a clue in (c): 'a fossil fuel such as coal'.

(b) (i) wind   (1)

> *Examiner's note*   Be careful to choose an answer here which you know
> something about and can write about in (ii).

  (ii) Wind turns blades of windmill   (1)
  which turn turbine to generate electricity.   (1)   (2)

> *Examiner's note*   You must link this answer to your choice in (i); state the
> *energy source* (wind/water/sun etc.) and *how it is converted* to electricity.

(c) Sun's energy is used in photosynthesis by plants which are eaten by
animals;   (1)
remains of animals and plants are changed into fossil fuels by action of
heat and pressure.   (1)   (2)

> *Examiner's note*   Try to state two clear facts here to gain the 2 marks.

(d) chemical $\longrightarrow$ heat   (1)
heat $\longrightarrow$ kinetic   (1)
kinetic $\longrightarrow$ electrical   (1)   (3)

> *Examiner's note*   You are asked for the energy transfers so write in the
> boxes the actual changes; for example movement (kinetic) $\longrightarrow$ electrical:
> the movement of the turbines produces electricity for the National Grid.

(Total marks 9)

Solutions
Forces and motion

Question 1

(a) (i) 3.5 ± 0.1 m/s (1)

> *Examiner's note* Look at the graph and locate 50 s on the horizontal (time) axis. Use a ruler to help you read off the velocity of about 3.5 m/s on the vertical axis. Don't forget to write the unit which is given on the axis.

(ii) 300 s (1)

> *Examiner's note* Look at where the velocity is zero. This is where Peter has stopped, after 300 seconds.

(iii) deceleration $= \dfrac{\text{change in velocity}}{\text{time}} = \dfrac{5}{10}$ (1)

$$= 0.5 \,(\text{m/s}^2) \quad (1) \qquad (2)$$

> *Examiner's note* At point X Peter's velocity is 5 m/s, then at Y it is 0. The change in velocity is therefore 5 m/s, over a period of 10 seconds (one small square on the grid = 10 seconds). Divide the change in velocity by the time in seconds and you have your answer, 0.5. The unit is written for you. You must show how you arrived at the answer so always include the formula if you can.

(iv) force $=$ mass $\times$ acceleration (1)
$= 60 \times 0.5 = 30$ N (1) (2)

> *Examiner's note* You need to know $F = m \times a$. You are told that Peter and his bicycle have a total mass of 60 kg. You have calculated his deceleration to be 0.5 m/s². So multiply 60×0.5 to find the answer 30 newtons. Don't forget the unit of force.

(b) (i) Friction between the tyre and the road. (1)

> *Examiner's note* Even if you cannot do part (a) (iv), it's worth going on to try part (b) (i). Friction makes the tyre and air feel warm.

(ii) As the air in the tyre warms up the particles move about more quickly; (1)
on colliding with the walls of the tyre the faster-moving particles exert a greater force. (1) (2)

(c) (i) Advantage: dynamo does not need replacing in the way batteries do, so cheaper to use. (1)
Disadvantage: when bicycle stops or slows down, the dynamo stops working. (1) (2)

> *Examiner's note* Even if you have never used a dynamo on a bicycle, you probably remember having to buy new batteries for a torch or something similar. The question tells you that the dynamo produces electricity when the wheel turns. You should be able to work out the disadvantages of the dynamo in that the lights will go out when the bicycle stops!

(ii) As the wheel (axle) turns the magnet rotates; (1)
a current is induced in the coil. (1) (2)

> *Examiner's note* The diagram should help you to obtain at least 1 mark here. You can see the cylindrical magnet attached to the axle.

(d) The current generated by the dynamo passes through diode Y;   (1)
the voltage produced (greater than that produced by the battery) causes the voltage drop (p.d.) across diode X to be in the wrong direction for conduction;   (1)
this prevents the flow of current through diode X; current flows from the dynamo through the lamp;   (1)
when the dynamo voltage decreases the voltage drop across X changes to the forward direction and current flows from the battery through X and the lamp.   (1)   (4)

Examiner's note   Look carefully at the circuit diagram and the information you are given in (d) to help you work out how this circuit works. Remember diodes allow current to flow only one way.

(Total marks 17)

Question 2

(a) Your diagram should show:
particles randomly arranged   (1)
more than 4 particles (up to about 12)   (1)   (2)

Examiner's note   Your diagram should show a liquid and therefore have more particles than Diagram A.

(b) Gases such as air can be compressed (squeezed).   (1)
When the driver pushes the pedal the air is compressed   (1)
and the pressure is not transmitted to the brakes: the brakes don't work.   (1)   (any 2 points)   (2)

Examiner's note   Read the information above the diagram of the braking system. The last sentence about liquids not being compressed will help you work out what happens when air gets in.

(Total marks 4)

Question 3 – student's answer

(a) Worn tyres have no tread and so would slide and skid on the road, there is very little friction between the tyre and the road so stopping distance is increased.

Examiner's note   Good – three logical points and you have stated that the stopping distance increases.   (3/3)

(b) (i) $v^2 = \dfrac{2 \times 242\,000}{1000}$

$v^2 = 484$

$v = 22\,m/s$

Examiner's note   Good – you have rearranged the formula and substituted the figures given correctly (kilojoules = 1000 joules). 1 mark has been given just for remembering to state the unit in your final answer.   (3/3)

(ii) Work done against braking force = k.e. lost = 242 000 J
Work = average force × distance so

$F = \dfrac{W}{d} = \dfrac{242\,000}{40} = 6050\,N$

Examiner's note   Good – always state the formula as this gains you 1 mark immediately, then substitute the figures.   (3/3)

Total score: 9/9

Examiner's note   Excellent!

Solutions
Waves

ANSWERS TO PRACTICE QUESTIONS

Question 1
(a) The line should go from X to the ear drum (A) to the bones to the cochlea (B) to the nerve endings (Y). (1)

> *Examiner's note* Use a good HB pencil to show the line from the sound waves at X to the nerve at Y.

(b) A ear drum (1)
   B cochlea (1) (2)

> *Examiner's note* This is where learning the labels on diagrams can gain you marks.

(c) (i) diagram C (1)
   (ii) diagram B (1) (2)

> *Examiner's note* The loudest sound has the greatest amplitude, shown in C; the highest pitch is shown by the waves being close together, in B.

(Total marks 5)

Question 2
(a) (i) 1. infra-red (1)
         2. ultra-violet (1) (2)

> *Examiner's note* Longer-wavelength radiation is refracted less by the prism.

   (ii) UV radiation is used for suntanning/fluorescence. (1)
        Microwaves are used for communication/cooking. (1) (2)

> *Examiner's note* Remember a few everyday examples.

(b) (i) Gamma rays (or X-rays). (1)
   (ii) The radiation kills the bacteria. (1)

> *Examiner's note* The word 'sterilize' is a clue to the answer.

(Total marks 6)

Question 3
(a) (i) sound ⟶ electrical (1)

   (ii) electrical ⟶ light (1)

> *Examiner's note* Read the information given and look at the diagram of the pupil producing sound. You are helped by the two boxes for your answers.

   (iii) transfers energy from one form to another (1)

> *Examiner's note* You are not asked for the specific conversion, only a general function.

(b) (i) amplitude B (1)
   (ii) peak E (1)
   (iii) trough D (1)
   (iv) wavelength A (1) (4)

> *Examiner's note* Try to think about a wave of water coming towards you; the trough and peak are easy to remember for 2 marks. The wavelength is the distance from one peak to the next.

(c) number of cycles per second   (1)

(d) (i)   reduce the amplitude   (1)
    (ii) reduce the frequency or increase the wavelength   (1)
          Examiner's note   The loudness of a sound is determined by its amplitude
          ('LA'); the pitch of a sound is determined by its frequency.

(e) The strings are moved by the fingers, plectrum or bow;   (1)
    the strings vibrate,   (1)
    the air inside the instrument vibrates;   (1)
    the vibrations cause longitudinal waves to travel through the surrounding
    air.   (1)   (4)
          Examiner's note   Try to visualise a guitar being played and think about the
          sequence of producing sound waves.

                                                                   (Total marks 14)

Question 4 – student's answer

(a) They are both transverse waves, they travel at the same speed.
          Examiner's note   Good, but take care – you are asked for one difference
          and you have given two similarities. You could have stated that they have
          different wavelength or frequency.   (1/2)

(b) (i)   Microwaves travel in straight lines so cannot go round the Earth.
          Examiner's note   Good, but better to state that the Earth is curved.   (2/2)

    (ii) If they spread out a bigger receiver dish would be needed.
          Examiner's note   Good – for the second mark describe the loss of power
          due to spreading.   (1/2)

(c) (i)

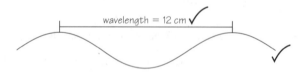

          Examiner's note   Good – a transverse wave is shown and you have marked
          the wavelength.   (2/2)

    (ii) Speed = frequency × wavelength

          $$f = \frac{300\,000\,000}{12} = 25\,000\,000 \text{ Hz}$$

          Examiner's note   The formula gains you a mark and another mark is
          awarded for correct working. However, you need to change 12 cm to 0.12 m
          – the correct answer is 2 500 000 000 Hz.   (3/4)

                                                                   Total score: 9/12

          Examiner's note   Well done.

Solutions
Radioactivity

ANSWERS TO PRACTICE QUESTIONS

Question 1

(a) Geiger-Müller tube (GM tube) (1)

(b) the building (1) the atmosphere (1) (2)

> *Examiner's note* Any two suggestions here: alternatives are soil, rocks.

(c) (i) alpha and beta (1)

(ii) Alpha was absorbed by the paper; (1)

beta was absorbed by the thin metal; (1)

no gamma was emitted because it would have passed through the thin metal. (1) (3)

> *Examiner's note* There is a lot to read in this question and a diagram and a table to look at. On the diagram it shows the radioactive isotope and the detector. You are told that materials are placed between the isotope and detector and the table shows how the count rate was reduced by the paper and the thin metal. Note that the count rate for background radiation is the same as that for thin and thick metal, showing that no gamma radiation is emitted from the isotope.

(d) Radiation from the isotope ionises (1)

the molecules in the cells of the skin (1)

and can damage the cells; (1)

the cells could multiply rapidly, leading to cancer. (1) (4)

> *Examiner's note* The main facts to remember here are that radiation damages cells and can cause cancer. You would gain 2 marks for these facts.

(e) (i) 27 protons (1) 33 neutrons (1) 27 electrons (1) (3)

> *Examiner's note* The information in the question tells you the proton number is 27. Subtract 27 from 60 (the mass number) and you have a neutron number of 33. The number of electrons = the number of protons.

(ii) Radiation kills the cancerous cells. (1)

> *Examiner's note* The information in (e)(ii) may also help you with part (d).

(Total marks 15)

Question 2

(a) (i) 1. Na is in group 1: it has one electron in its outer shell. (1)

2. The outer electron is loosely bound so Na readily forms a positive ion Na$^+$. (1)

3. The outer electrons become 'free' from the positive ions. (1) (3)

> *Examiner's note* Remember that the elements in the first column on the left side of the table are the alkali metals. Try to write three reasons which the alkali metals have in common, rather than properties of sodium.

(ii) The sodium atom is larger than the lithium atom (1)

so the outer electron of sodium is further away from the nucleus (1)

and so the outer electron is more readily lost. (1) (3)

> *Examiner's note* Remember that as you move down a group the size of atom increases although the atoms have the same number of electrons in their outer shell. The further away from the attraction of the nucleus the more likely the electron can be lost and so the more reactive the atom.

(b) (i) accurate plot of points (1) smooth curve (1) (2)

Examiner's note You are told the half-life is 15 hours. Start with a point at 100% at time 0 and then plot 50% at 15 hours. The percentage of radioactive isotope has halved in 15 hours. The percentage falls to 25% after another 15 hours and then to 12.5% after another 15 hours. You are given the axes and scale here so all that is necessary is a plot of the data.

(ii) construction lines shown on grid paper (1)

calculation: $\dfrac{10 \times \text{reading from graph}}{100}$ (1)

answer = figure from above (no units required) (1) (3)

Examiner's note From your graph draw construction lines across and upwards to read off the percentage of radioactive isotope after 40 hours. It may be about 16–18%. Multiply your answer by 10 (grams) and divide by 100. Your answer should be around 1.7 g, but it will depend on the accuracy of your graph.

(c) positively charged helium ions (1) electrons (1) (2)

(d) (i) $^{238}_{94}\text{Pu}$ (plutonium) (1) because it has the longest half-life. (1) (2)

(ii) Cobalt-60 releases gamma radiation which can penetrate the body and kill cancer cells. (1)

Gamma radiation could damage healthy tissue inside the body if used to treat skin cancer. (1)

Phosphorus-32 releases beta radiation which only affects skin cells. (1) (3)

Examiner's note The information you need to answer this question is contained in the table in (d). You need to re-interpret the facts.

(Total marks 18)

Question 3 – student's answer

(a)

Type of radiation	What is it?	What type of charge does it carry?
Alpha	A helium nucleus ✓	Negative ✗
Beta	Electron	Negative
Gamma	E.M. radiation ✓	No charge ✓

Examiner's note An alternative answer to *Alpha/What is it?* is '2 neutrons and 2 protons'. You have one wrong answer – an alpha particle carries a *positive* charge. (3/4)

(b) (i) The one with half-life 6 minutes wouldn't last long enough. The one with half-life 6 days may give too much radiation. The doctor uses a gamma emitter because alpha and beta rays wouldn't penetrate the body.

Examiner's note Good – two clear points given in the first two sentences. However, read the question to see what other information has been given. Alpha and beta rays are absorbed by the body, damaging cells, whereas gamma rays are not absorbed and so reach the detector. (3/4)

(ii) 6400 is halved to 3200 after 6 hours

3200 is halved to 1600 after 6 hours

1600 is halved to 800 after 6 hours

800 is halved to 400 after 6 hours

Examiner's note Yes, 24 hours is 4 half-lives each of 6 hours, so $\frac{1}{2} \times \frac{1}{2} \times \frac{1}{2} \times \frac{1}{2} \times 6400 = 400$. (2/2)

(iii) Background radiation.

Examiner's note Good, but also remember that decay is a random process so the count rate will not be exact. (1/2)

Good. Total score: 9/12

This practice paper consists of nine typical GCSE questions across the three areas: Sc 2 *Life processes and living things*, Sc 3 *Materials and their properties*, and Sc 4 *Physical processes*. In the real exam there would be three papers, each based on one of Sc 2, Sc 3 and Sc 4, and with 5 to 14 questions, depending on the length of questions. Most of the exam papers carry about 90 to 100 marks for about $1\frac{1}{2}$ hours of examination time. This practice paper carries 82 marks and is designed to take you about 1 hour 15 minutes.

When you have completed the paper, go through each answer carefully against the marking guidelines together with the examiner's comments. It is difficult to say what overall mark would equal a particular grade, as these decisions are made at meetings of senior examiners each year and are based on the difficulty of a particular paper and how the questions were answered. A very approximate guideline for this paper would be about 60–65 marks minimum needed for a grade A; about 48—53 marks minimum for a grade C; and 35–40 minimum for a grade E – but it must be stressed that these are approximate figures only.

PRACTICE PAPER

Time allowed: 1 hour 15 minutes

Instructions to candidates

▶ Answer *all* the questions in the spaces provided in this book.
▶ Show all stages in any calculations and state the units.
▶ Write all your answers in blue or black ink or ball-point pen.

Information for candidates

▶ The number of marks is given in brackets at the end of each part-question.
▶ Marks will not be deducted for incorrect answers.
▶ You are reminded of the importance of clear English and orderly presentation in your answers.

Question 1

(a) Diagrams A, B, C and D show blood vessels and a sweat gland in the skin.

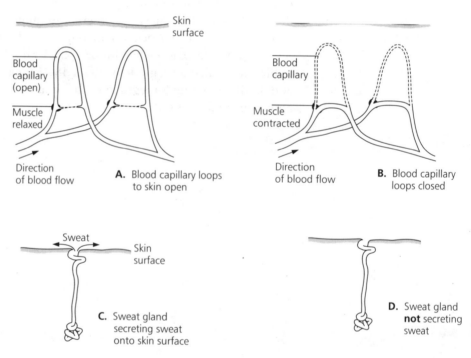

(i) Which *two* diagrams show the blood vessels and the sweat gland when the body is reducing heat loss from the skin?

.... and ....(1)

(ii) Explain how sweating helps to cool the skin.

....

....

....

....

....(2)

(b) In an investigation into temperature control a person was kept in a room maintained at a temperature of 45°C. The graph shows the effect of the person eating a mouthful of ice on the temperature of the skin and of the blood.

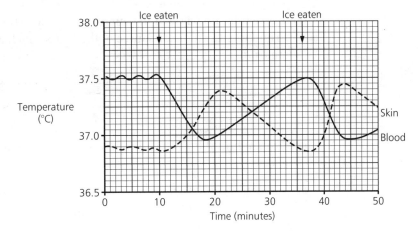

(i) Give *two* changes, other than skin temperature, which will occur in the body in response to the change in blood temperature after eating the ice.

1. ....

2. ....(2)

(ii) Explain why the skin temperature changes after eating the ice.

....

....

....

....(2)

(Total marks 7)

NEAB

Question 2

The pie chart shows the proportions of 'greenhouse gas' emissions during the 1980s. The table shows the relative warming potential of these 'greenhouse gases'.

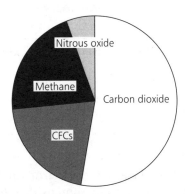

'Greenhouse gas'	Global warming potential (over 100 years)
Carbon dioxide	1
Methane	11
Nitrous oxide	270
CFCs	3400–7100

*CFCs are chlorofluorocarbons
Data supplied by Worldwide Fund for Nature (WWF).*

(a) (i) Which of the 'greenhouse gases' was released in the greatest amount during the 1980s?

....

(ii) Predict which of the gases released during the 1980s is likely to have the greatest warming effect over the next 100 years.

....(1)

(b) Give *one* possible reason why the concentration of nitrous oxide in the atmosphere has increased greatly since the early part of this century.

....

....(1)

(c) There were no CFCs in the atmosphere before the 1930s. Suggest why this is so and identify a major source of the CFCs which are now present in the atmosphere.

....

....

....(2)

(d) Explain how the gases shown in the table can bring about the 'greenhouse effect'.

....

....

....

....

....(4)

(Total marks 9)

London

Question 3

The diagram represents the arrangement of electrons in a magnesium atom.

Magnesium atom

(a) Complete the table.

	Number of			Electron arrangement
	Protons	Neutrons	Electrons	
Magnesium-24				2,8,2
Oxygen-16		8	8	

(3)

(b) Magnesium oxide contains ionic bonding.

Explain fully, in terms of transfer of electrons and the formation of ions, the changes which occur when magnesium oxide is formed from magnesium and oxygen atoms.

....

....

....

....(4)

(c) Sodium chloride and magnesium oxide have similar crystal structures and both contain ionic bonding. The melting points of sodium chloride and magnesium oxide are 800°C and 2800°C respectively.

Suggest why the melting point of magnesium oxide is much higher than the melting point of sodium chloride.

(Sodium chloride contains Na⁺ and Cl⁻ ions.)

....

....

....

....(3)

(Total marks 10)

MEG

Question 4

(a) The diagram below shows the cross-section of an aerosol can containing a deodorant.

(i) Explain how the deodorant spray is formed when the aerosol valve is pressed.

....

....

....

....(3)

(ii) When the deodorant evaporates quickly from the skin why does the skin feel cool?

....

....(1)

(b) By changing the pressure of gas in an aerosol can, different mixtures are produced as shown in the table.

Mixture	Pressure of gas	Example
Fine droplets	High	Air freshener
Larger droplets	Medium	Hair spray
Foam	Low	Shaving foam

Use the table above to suggest how shaving foam is formed.

....

....

....(2)

(c) Explain, in terms of particles, why it is dangerous to put aerosol cans on a bonfire.

....

....

....

....(3)

(Total marks 9)

London

Question 5

Zinc oxide is made by reacting zinc gas with air. Hot zinc gas reacts with oxygen from the air to make the zinc oxide.

(a) Write a word equation for this reaction.

....(1)

(b) Use the kinetic theory to explain why energy must be supplied to the particles of zinc to change the zinc from solid to gas.

....

....

....(2)

(c) How could you make the zinc evaporate faster?

....

....(1)

(d) Apart from the cost of the zinc, suggest *one* other major cost of this process.

....

....(1)

(Total marks 5)

NEAB

Question 6

The theory of plate tectonics suggests that:

the crust of the Earth is made up of plates;

the plates move at various speeds and in various directions.

(a) Give *three* features that may be observed at the plate boundaries.

1.   ....

2.   ....

3.   ....(3)

(b) What causes the Earth's plates to move? Explain your answer.

....

....

....

....

....

....(4)

(c) Geologists studied the rocks either side of the plate boundary in the middle of the Atlantic. They found that the rocks had an interesting magnetic pattern.

White stripes: reversely magnetised (S)
Black stripes: normally magnetised (N)

This magnetic pattern gave good evidence for the theory that the continents do move apart. Explain how.

....

....

....

....(3)

(Total marks 10)

SEG

Question 7

This shows two types of household lamp.

100 W
filament lamp

23 W
electronic lamp

The lamps each give out light at the same rate when connected to the mains 230 V supply.

(a) Calculate the current in the 23 W lamp when connected to the mains supply.

....amps   (3)

(b) In the filament lamp, current passes through a metal (tungsten) wire. The current in the electronic lamp passes through mercury vapour.

Describe the similarities and difference in the way that current passes in the lamps.

....

....

....

....

....

....(4)

(c) Explain how the term '230 V' describes the energy transfer in the lamps.

....

....(1)

(Total marks 8)

MEG

Question 8

The graph shows how the braking distance of a car in good condition depends on the speed at which it is travelling.

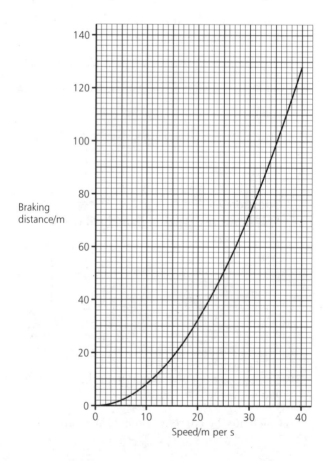

(a) (i) Is it true to say that 'if speed is doubled the braking distance is also doubled'? Use data from the graph to support your answer.

....

....(2)

(ii) Explain why the braking distance at a speed of 60 m/s would be 288 m.

....

....

....(3)

(iii) The driver of a car travelling at 25 m/s suddenly notices a person stepping into the road, and applies the brakes.

Explain why the total stopping distance is greater than 50 m.

....

....

....(2)

(b) A car travelling at 20 m/s takes 32 m to stop.

Its average speed during braking is 10 m/s.

Use this information to calculate the time it takes to stop a car from a speed of 20 m/s.

....

....

....

....

....(3)

(c)

800 kg (driver only)   1200 kg (driver, passengers and luggage)

(i) The braking force on the car is 4000 N.

Calculate the deceleration of the car when there is only the driver in it.

....

deceleration: .... unit: ....   (4)

(ii) Explain why the braking distance of the fully loaded car will be greater than the car with the driver alone, when they are both travelling at the same speed.

....

....

....

....

....(3)

(Total marks 17)

MEG

Question 9

(a) The diagram below shows a cross-section of the human eye.

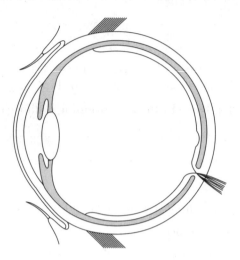

(i) Which *two* parts of the eye are used to focus the incoming light?

1. ....

2. ....(2)

(ii) Describe how the image formed on the retina, by a normal eye, compares
with the object seen.

....

....(2)

(b) Diagrams A, B, C and D below show four different eyes receiving light. In
diagrams A and B light comes from a very distance object, while in diagrams
C and D the light comes from a near object.

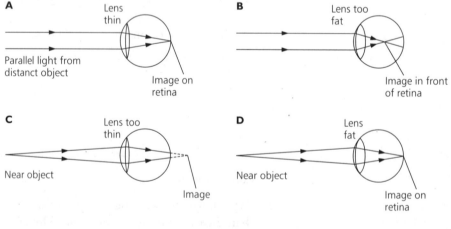

(i) Which *two* diagrams show a normal eye?

.... and ....

(ii) Which diagram shows an eye suffering from short sight?

....

(iii) Which diagram shows an eye suffering from long sight?

....   (3)

(Total marks 7)

NEAB

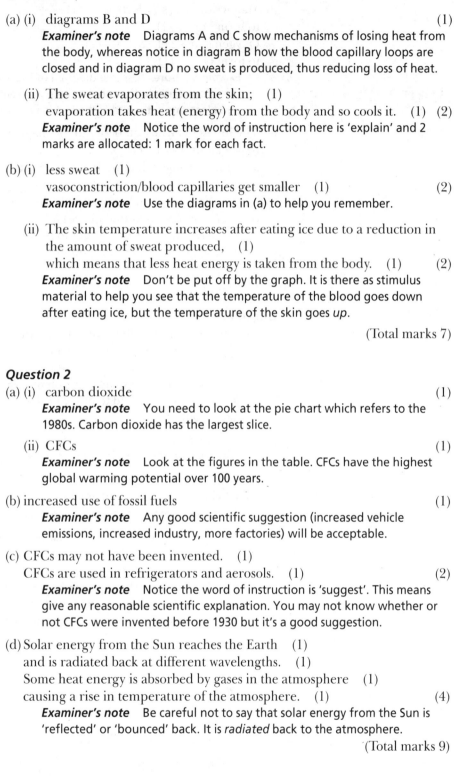

ANSWERS TO TIMED PRACTICE PAPER

Question 1

(a) (i)   diagrams B and D   (1)

Examiner's note   Diagrams A and C show mechanisms of losing heat from the body, whereas notice in diagram B how the blood capillary loops are closed and in diagram D no sweat is produced, thus reducing loss of heat.

   (ii) The sweat evaporates from the skin;   (1)
         evaporation takes heat (energy) from the body and so cools it.   (1)   (2)

Examiner's note   Notice the word of instruction here is 'explain' and 2 marks are allocated: 1 mark for each fact.

(b) (i)   less sweat   (1)
         vasoconstriction/blood capillaries get smaller   (1)   (2)

Examiner's note   Use the diagrams in (a) to help you remember.

   (ii) The skin temperature increases after eating ice due to a reduction in the amount of sweat produced,   (1)
         which means that less heat energy is taken from the body.   (1)   (2)

Examiner's note   Don't be put off by the graph. It is there as stimulus material to help you see that the temperature of the blood goes down after eating ice, but the temperature of the skin goes *up*.

                                                                   (Total marks 7)

Question 2

(a) (i)   carbon dioxide   (1)

Examiner's note   You need to look at the pie chart which refers to the 1980s. Carbon dioxide has the largest slice.

   (ii) CFCs   (1)

Examiner's note   Look at the figures in the table. CFCs have the highest global warming potential over 100 years.

(b) increased use of fossil fuels   (1)

Examiner's note   Any good scientific suggestion (increased vehicle emissions, increased industry, more factories) will be acceptable.

(c) CFCs may not have been invented.   (1)
    CFCs are used in refrigerators and aerosols.   (1)   (2)

Examiner's note   Notice the word of instruction is 'suggest'. This means give any reasonable scientific explanation. You may not know whether or not CFCs were invented before 1930 but it's a good suggestion.

(d) Solar energy from the Sun reaches the Earth   (1)
    and is radiated back at different wavelengths.   (1)
    Some heat energy is absorbed by gases in the atmosphere   (1)
    causing a rise in temperature of the atmosphere.   (1)   (4)

Examiner's note   Be careful not to say that solar energy from the Sun is 'reflected' or 'bounced' back. It is *radiated* back to the atmosphere.

                                                                   (Total marks 9)

Question 3

(a) magnesium-24   12 protons, 12 neutrons, 12 electrons
    oxygen-16   8 protons, electron arrangement 2, 6   (3)

Examiner's note   There is a lot of help given in the table and the diagram. Count the number of electrons in the diagram of magnesium (12). The number of protons is the same. The number of neutrons is 24 − 12. The number of protons in oxygen is the same as the number of electrons (8); or you can work it out from 16 − 8. The arrangement of electrons in magnesium will give you a hint to the electron arrangement in oxygen; always fill up the shells closest to the nucleus. All five answers in the table must be correct for 3 marks. If you make a mistake you lose a mark!

(b) Magnesium loses 2 electrons   (1)
to form Mg^{2+}. (1)
Oxygen gains 2 electrons   (1)
to form O^{2-}.   (1)   (4)
Examiner's note   Use the diagram of the arrangement of electrons and the information in the table to help you remember that magnesium has two electrons in the outer shell which are lost when an ion is formed.

(c) The forces of attraction between the magnesium ions (Mg^{2+}) and the oxygen ions (O^{2-})   (1)
are much stronger than between the sodium ions (Na^+) and the chlorine ions (Cl^-);   (1)
more energy is needed to overcome these forces and so the melting point of magnesium oxide is higher.   (1)   (3)
Examiner's note   Don't forget to relate your answer to the different melting points of the two substances.

(Total marks 10)

Question 4

(a) (i)   The pressure inside is greater than the pressure outside;   (1)
the propellant exerts pressure on the liquid,   (1)
forcing the liquid out when the valve is opened.   (1)   (3)
Examiner's note   Use the labels on the diagram to help you work out how the spray is formed and to give you words such as 'valve', 'pressure' and 'propellant'.

(ii) The process of evaporation takes heat energy from the skin.   (1)
Examiner's note   This is a similar process to cooling down by sweating.

(b) A foam is bubbles of gas dispersed in a liquid   (1)
which need low pressure to expand.   (1)   (2)
Examiner's note   The information about low pressure is in the table.

(c) As the temperature in the can increases   (1)
the pressure in the can increases; (1)
the can explodes as molecules cannot escape.   (1)   (3)
Examiner's note   The explanation is that the propellant molecules vaporise and so there are more collisions with the sides of the container, so the pressure increases. However, a concise clear answer will gain full marks!

(Total marks 9)

Question 5

(a) zinc + oxygen $\longrightarrow$ zinc oxide   (1)
Examiner's note   Look carefully at the information given above the diagram. You are told that *zinc...* reacts with *oxygen...* to make *zinc oxide*.

(b) Energy must be supplied to make the particles move faster   (1)
and overcome forces of attraction between the particles.   (1)   (2)
Examiner's note   Remember the particles are already moving and need to move more.

(c) increase the temperature   (1)

(d) cost of heating the furnace   (1)
Examiner's note   Any suitable suggestion, such as cost of transport of raw materials, would gain the mark.

(Total marks 5)

Question 6

(a) 1. volcanoes   (1)
   2. earthquakes   (1)
   3. ocean ridges   (1)   (3)
   Examiner's note   It is when the plates are moving in relation to each other that volcanoes and earthquakes occur.

(b) The plates float on the mantle   (1)
   which is molten;   (1)
   radioactive elements in the mantle give off heat,   (1)
   setting up convection currents.   (1)   (4)
   Examiner's note   This is all quite difficult and is really only needed for A/A* grades. You can still attempt to gain 1 or 2 marks even if you cannot score the maximum!

(c) The Earth's magnetic field has undergone reversals of polarity;   (1)
   the magnetic pattern shown is the same on both sides of the gap;   (1)
   could be explained by molten magma rising up and pushing plates apart.   (1)   (3)
   Examiner's note   You are given a clue under the diagram that the stripes are due to reversed polarity.

(Total marks 10)

Question 7

(a) current $= \dfrac{\text{power}}{\text{voltage}}$ (1)

   $= \dfrac{23\,(W)}{230\,(V)}$ (1)

   $= 0.1\,(A)$ (1)   (3)
   Examiner's note   When you see the word 'calculate' remember to state the formula to gain a mark. The figures for power and voltage are given in the question, as are the units.

(b) The current in each is due to the movement of charged particles;   (1)
   negative charges (electrons) move in the tungsten wire   (1)
   in one direction;   (1)
   positive ions and negative electrons move in the gas   (1)
   in both directions   (1)   (max 4)
   Examiner's note   Look carefully at the question. You are asked for similarities and differences between the two lamps. The first point on the above list is the similarity and you are given a clue to this point in (b): 'the current passes'.

(c) 230 joules of energy is transferred for each coulomb of charge which passes.   (1)
   Examiner's note   In the lamps 230 joules of electrical energy is being transferred (converted) into heat and light.

(Total marks 8)

Question 8

(a) (i) No, at 20 m/s the braking distance is about 32 m
      but at 40 m/s the braking distance is 128 m.   (2)
      Examiner's note   In your answer make reference to actual data given. Choose two speeds, one double the other and read off the braking distances from the graph.

   (ii) The braking distance at 30 m/s is 72 m   (1)
      so at 60 m/s it is 288 m   (1)
      since the braking distance quadruples when the speed is doubled.   (1) (3)
      Examiner's note   You are given some of this information in the question and on the graph.

(iii) The driver takes time to respond to the person on the road; (1)
during this thinking time the car will move some distance before
braking. (1) (2)

(b) time taken $= \dfrac{\text{distance}}{\text{average speed}}$ (1)

$= \dfrac{32\,\text{m}}{10\,\text{m/s}}$ (1)

$= 3.2\,\text{s}$ (1) (3)

Examiner's note Insert the figures into the formula; the car takes 32
metres to stop at an average speed of 10 m/s.

(c) (i) acceleration $= \dfrac{\text{force}}{\text{mass}}$ (1)

deceleration of car $= \dfrac{4000\,(\text{N})}{800\,(\text{kg})}$ (1)

$= 5$ (1) m/s^2 (1) (4)

Examiner's note Insert the figures given in the question into the formula.
You are given 1 mark for stating the formula and also 1 mark for the
correct units. The units are used elsewhere in the question so look for clues!

(ii) The fully loaded car has a greater mass (1)
so its deceleration will be smaller (1)
and it will take longer to stop. (1) (3)

Examiner's note You are given clues in the diagrams of the two cars to
help you in answering this. The fully loaded car has a mass of 1200 kg.

(Total marks 17)

Question 9

(a) (i) 1. cornea (1)
2. lens (1) (2)

Examiner's note You are not often required to draw complete diagrams
of organs such as the eye and ear but you do need to learn the names and
functions of the parts.

(ii) The image on the retina is smaller (1)
and it is inverted (upside down). (1) (2)

(b) (i) diagrams A and D (1)

Examiner's note Look at diagrams A and D where the light rays meet *on*
the retina; these are the normal eyes. You need to give both diagrams for
the mark.

(ii) diagram B (1)

Examiner's note The light rays from a distant object meet in front of the
retina; the person would be short-sighted.

(iii) diagram C (1) (3)

Examiner's note The light rays from a near object meet behind the retina;
the person would be long-sighted.

(Total marks 7)